The Mansions of Long Island's Gold Coast

To Diane
  + Bob

Happy Easter
  with love
    Mom + Dad 1997

The Mansions
of Long Island's
Gold Coast

BY MONICA RANDALL

RIZZOLI
NEW YORK

Dedicated to
CHARLES VAN MAANEN

Revised, enlarged edition first published in
the United States of America in 1987 by
Rizzoli International Publications, Inc.

Library of Congress Cataloging-in-Publication Data
Randall, Monica.
  The Mansions of Long Island's Gold Coast.

  Bibliography: p.
  Includes index.
  1. Mansions—New York (State)—Long Island.
2. Historic buildings—New York (State)—
Long Island.   3. Long Island (N.Y.)—Biography.
4. Long Island (N.Y.)—Social life and customs.
5. Architecture, Domestic—New York (State)—
Long Island.   I. Title.
F127.L8R23   1987   974.7′21   86–31558
ISBN 0–8478–0821–1 (pbk.)

Printed and bound in Hong Kong

Contents

Foreword

As a child I played among the ruins of abandoned mansions along Long Island's "Gold Coast" and would make them, depending on the play of the day, into my childhood visions of castles and forts. But as I grew older and started hearing the real stories of those grand buildings I realized that my imagination could never match the reality of the splendid living their walls once held. As a teenager I started photographing as many of the mansions that I could possibly visit and became almost obsessed with their history, mysteries and legends. For the past fifteen years I have searched out and talked with hundreds of people who were once part of the lost world these homes represent: the butlers, grooms, gatekeepers, chamber maids and many of the Grandes Dames who once held court in marble ballrooms and manicured gardens. Their stories of the life in these very exclusive domains, their reminiscences of little-known customs and codes of protocol and their anecdotes of often bizarre events has given me a unique view into a way of life in the not too distant past that is too rapidly becoming forgotten. This book is a sum of their memories and of my fascination with these majestic homes.

Oyster Bay, N.Y.   MONICA RANDALL

Acknowledgments

On the many visits to North Shore mansions to obtain information and photographs for this book, I have received much cooperation and support from the owners of homes, newspaper people, foundation officials, archivists and librarians. My deepest gratitude is expressed to all and special thanks to Daian Frese and Peggy Katzander who made the unreadable, readable.

Mrs. Altman, Bryant Park Library, Roslyn
Mr. Anthony, Old Westbury Gardens
Mr. Harvey Aronson
Mrs. Elizabeth Babcock of Woodbury
Mr. George F. Baker, II
Mr. Chris Bodom
Mrs. Dorothy Borges
Mr. John Bralower
Brookville Police Dept., Lieutenant Smith
Mr. Michel Canjero, of Peacock Point
Mr. Stewart W. Carter, C. W. Post Library
Mr. & Mrs. Pat Carucchi
Mrs. Nina Clairborne
Mr. John Davis, of Pembroke
Mrs. Dorothy Davison
Mr. Bud De Gonzogue of Dodge Sloan Estate
Mr. John B. DeJesu
Mr. Bill Donalson, New York Inst. of Technology
Ms. Dorothy Dranow
Eastern Military Academy
Mrs. Dorothy Fordyce
Mr. & Mrs. Jack Friedus
Mr. Glen Giwojna
Mr. & Mrs. Douglas Griffin, of Baker Estate
Mrs. C. Z. Guest
Heckscher Museum
Mr. Ted Hefner of Oak Knoll
Mrs. Hersh, of Chimneys
Huntington Historical Society
Mrs. Dane Johnson, of Meudon (for the 1909 photos by August Patzig)
Mrs. Marion Johnson
Mr. Howard Katzander
Mr. Robert King
Ms. Shelly G. King
Mr. Robert Koch
Mr. & Mrs. Lemke, Welwyn
The Locust Valley Leader
Mrs. William Long
Long Island Heritage Magazine
Long Island Press
Mrs. K. L. Luckenback
Mr. Melvin Luebke, of Mill Neck Manor

Mr. John Maddacks
Manhasset Chamber of Commerce
Manhasset Library
Mansions & Millionairs Inc.
Mr. Richard Markoll, Woolworth Estate
Mr. Esmond Martin
Mr. Bob Mckay of S.P.L.I.A.
Mrs. Joseph McMullan
Mr. Samuel Mitchell
Nassau County Dept. of Recreatiuon & Parks, Ms. Gloria Roccio
Mr. Winchi, Nassau Historical Society
Mr. Ray Nau
Newsday, Library staff, and Marilyn Goldstein and Stan Green
New York Inst. of Technology, Mr. Bill Donalson, Mrs. Kaufmann, and Dr. A. Schure
William Nimmo, North Shore Preservation Society
Mrs. F. Florence Norris
Mr. Grover O'Neal
Oyster Bay Gardian, Mrs. Edwena Snow
Mrs. Paul Pennoyer
Mrs. Nancy Pirtel (for Zog photos)
Planting Fields Arboretum, Mrs. James & Mr. Jones
Brother Roman, St. Francis Monastery
Roslyn Historical Landmark Society
Mr. John C. Ryan
Mr. John Samuels III
Mr. & Mrs. Alex Scheriff
Mr. & Mrs. Robert C. Schuler
Mr. Frederick Woodbury Schwerin, Jr.
Mr. Augusta Shera
Mr. Edward Smits
Mr. & Mrs. Leonard Sonnenburg
Mr. Lewis Steall
Mr. Harry Stanley Sucharski
Mr. & Mrs. Bronson Trevor
Mr. Charles Van Maanen
Peter Van Santvoord
Dr. Woodford
Mr. & Mrs. Thomas & Alicia Zizzo

The Mansions of
Long Island's Gold Coast

BEACON TOWERS BUILT BY AUGUST BELMONT AT SANDS POINT IS THE HOUSE WHICH
INSPIRED SCOTT FITZGERALD TO WRITE *THE GREAT GATSBY*

GATSBY'S LONG ISLAND,
"The Gold Coast"

Perhaps the most lavish parties ever held in the pages of American literature were the galas Jay Gatsby threw at his estate on Long Island's North Shore. It was the "Gold Coast" when it glittered, a time of elegance and splendor, gilded ceilings, private yachts, castles surrounded by polo fields, marble pavilions, and formal gardens.

The original Gatsby mansion that inspired F. Scott Fitzgerald has long since been bulldozed and replaced by split levels, but many other mansions remain hidden behind tightly closed gates, forgotten relics of an era whose social pillars are fast eroding. This book deals with the untold story of the heyday between the two World Wars, and the tragedy of what has become of the grandeur and the huge estates that were once the playground for glamourous society gatherings.

Less than one hour's drive from midtown Manhattan are found the abandoned remains of a lost world. Today in a state of ruin and decay, they are looked upon as white elephants and are largely uninhabited and often crumbling. Some have been empty since the crash of 'Twenty-nine; others are doomed to be bulldozed within the year. Often they are held for back taxes by various banks while builders bid for the choice land to construct their rows and rows of monotonous split levels.

Great legends have grown up around the Gold Coast; they began when substantial fortunes were made from the many expanding industries, just after the turn of the century. Then William K. Vanderbilt drew world-wide attention to the area by initiating the Vanderbilt Cup races in 1904. Soon men like F. W. Woolworth, J. P. Morgan, Harry P. Whitney, Otto Kahn, and Daniel Guggenheim the copper king, and their great wealth and power led in time to an architectural phenomenon unparalleled both in extensiveness and originality. Built without financial restrictions, castles, Italian villas, and French châteaux began to sprout up along the coast of Long Island Sound. The formal gardens were landscaped to match the magnificence of the historical castles and palatial residences of Europe's legendary lands. They were constructed before the days of heavy taxes, within a concentrated area stretching from Manhasset to Huntington, and as far south as the polo center in Old Westbury.

The millionaires and tycoons with their newly amassed fortunes indulged their every whim in trying to outdo their friends and business rivals. Lavish parties were held, and as F. Scott Fitzgerald depicted in his book, *The Great Gatsby*,

> It was a time elegantly dressed men and women came and went like moths among the whisperings, champagne and the stars, where guests dived from the tower of his float during the day and his motorboats drew aquaplanes over the swirling wavelets of the Sound, and in the evening the orchestra arrived and played cocktail music and the motorcars were parked five deep in the driveway, and the halls were gaudy with color and bouncy with noise. Gay young women were surrounded by men in tuxedos, and there were eddies of conversation and splashes of laughter, and corks popped and liquor flowed, and you knew it was a time that would never come again.

Mrs. Charles Payson's gala costume balls were legendary, given around the enormous Olympic size pool at her Manhasset estate; the pool was surrounded by classic white pillars connected by pale blue treillaged walls from which hung hundreds of colorful Chinese lanterns. There were huge urns filled with flaming torches, and dozens of pastel colored lights played off the lace-like walls and lavishly costumed guests who danced away the night to a calypso band she had flown up from Havana for the evening. To add to the magic, there were swans floating in the pool, with flowers and candles to dazzle as many as two hundred guests.

The social climax of the era came in 1924 when the Prince of Wales, the world's most eligible bachelor, came to Nassau County to visit and attend the polo matches in Old Westbury. The North Shore became almost obsessed with the Prince: the members of its élite stretched their imaginations to the fullest in an effort to lure the future King of England to their parties. He was guest of honor at some of the country's most glittering balls. The most famous of them was given by Clarence Mackay, the heir to the $500,000,000 telegraph and cable fortune made by his father, John W. Mackay. Twelve hundred prominent guests filled the ballroom at Harbor Hill, Mackay's six-million-dollar, fifty-two room castle in Roslyn. The trees bordering the mile-long drive up to the mansion sparkled with thousands of blue lights. Breathtaking fountains were aglow with more lights, while on the grand marquee the music of Paul Whiteman's band played into the night. At one point the much sought after Prince became weary of all the stuffy formality and protocol and is said to have slipped away one night from one to five A.M. No one knows of his whereabouts at that time, though rumor has it that he was driven to a secluded boathouse in Cold Spring Harbor where he, longing to be just like regular folk, drank with friends and visiting Ziegfeld showgirls.

Contrary to the image of high society, it was the fad of the day for lady guests to fling their lingerie to the winds as they passed the gates upon leaving. Local folk still recall seeing chauffeurs ceremoniously retrieving their ladies' undergarments in the wee hours of the morning. There was another bash given at Harbor Hill to honor Charles Lindbergh following his historic ticker tape parade in New York City. So exhausted was he that arriving at the gala he walked in the front door and slipped out the back door without saying a word. Everyone who was anybody gave parties, the more

GLITTERING PARTIES WERE HELD IN AND AROUND THE MOSAIC AND
GOLD SWIMMING POOL AT PEMBROKE

outrageous the better. Bradley Martin gave a "Come in the most expensive costume you
can devise" party, given at the height of the Depression. Mrs. Charles Payson was known
for her lavish costume balls, and at one bash there were the famous Flora Dora Girls

THE OTTO KAHN ESTATE

dancing through the halls to delight the guests, and circus horses performing on the lawn. Endless rounds of coming-out parties were given under pink and white tents, festooned with masses of orange blossoms, fluttering ribbons and flowers draped over arcades of trellises.

Hollywood Stars Come to Long Island

In time the Hollywood film stars built their share of mini-mansions; among them were Ed Wynn, Groucho Marx, Ring Lardner, Basil Rathbone, Lew Fields, Leslie Howard, and Eddie Cantor. Before the crash of 1929 there were over five hundred of these Flapper Age mansions on Long Island's North Shore. Fewer than half of those exist today. There were other extravagances which can never be duplicated: Otto Kahn, who made millions in the stock market, was determined to have his French château placed on the highest "mountain" Long Island had to offer, but alas, it was occupied. Undaunted, Kahn and his army of builders spent two years raising the height of the unoccupied hill he had found. The 125-room château was then placed on the man-made mountain, and contained a dining room with ample room for two hundred dinner guests.

Not to be outdone by other party givers, Kahn gave a yearly Easter Party on the lawns of his 600-acre estate. To differentiate his Easter Egg hunt from those of the common folk, Kahn made sure that each egg contained a one thousand dollar bill. The colorful eggs were then hidden in the gardens and behind every bush. One can only assume that this was one of the most popular events of the year, even to the North Shore nobility.

There were many other families playing on Long Island's Gold Coast, well-known and not-so-well-known. With one's wealth came the need for, indeed the necessity of, outdoing one's peers socially. Some imported entire castles, stone by stone; one came complete with a drawbridge and moat, where playful alligators eyed the arriving guests in the hope that one might "drop in for lunch." After Mrs. August Belmont's castle, Beacon Towers, was completed, she decided to visit Scotland's Blair Castle, the centuries-old domain of the Duke of Atholl. She is said to have remarked upon seeing it, "My dear, my castle in Sands Point, U.S.A. is far more authentic!"

There were other indulgences of personal foibles besides Morgan's cows, Guggenheim's frogs, and Kahn's Easter Eggs: there was Mackay's moose—Clarence and his friends practiced marksmanship as they aimed at an electrically operated stuffed moose, complete with antlers, that ran on a track outside a secluded log cabin on his Roslyn estate. To carry the theme even further, inside the reception hall he had a suit of armor mounted on a stuffed horse. One of the curious fancies of Mrs. Paul Prybal, who had an estate in Lattingtown, was her passion for mice. She had mice everywhere. Scattered about on her night table there was a vast collection of porcelain figurines of the long tailed creatures. Mice were embroidered on her linens and used as a motif throughout the elegant house, much to her husband's dismay. I am told that she also fancied cows and had a fine herd of them grazing about the spacious lawns. Rumor has it that her husband was known to climb to the top of the barn silo with his shotgun and take pot shots at the cows as his way of warding off stress.

THE STABLES AT CASTLE GOULD

THE HOME OF J. P. MORGAN

J. P. Morgan himself carried the standard for the Morgan family with a whole island off Glen Cove, complete with armed guards, who from the guard house that stood at the entrance to his own private bridge watched for foe. To simplify tending the garden, Morgan had a herd of cows to mow the front lawn. Copper brought a great fortune to Daniel Guggenheim, who bought a 125-room feudal castle, a replica of Ireland's Kilkenny Castle, the ancestral home of the Marquis of Armond. The stable of his "Castle Gould" to this day contains a carousel complete with horses, zebras and huge green frogs to delight his house guests.

Prohibition

When Prohibition struck, the parties got even wilder, as stills were set up in the basements of the estates, and rum-running became the rage. No Long Island party ever ran dry. The long coal tunnels that ran from the Sound up to the basements' massive heating systems had been used to bring in the coal off the barges by small railroad cars. Now they became the hiding places of bootleggers who used them to smuggle their contraband booze. Oak Point in Bayville made headlines at the height of Prohibition when a raging storm caused a huge yacht to crash upon the rocks of the private estate. The infamous *William T. Bell* was disguised as a vessel carrying lumber, but in fact it was loaded with barrels of Scotch whiskey. Soon it was all over town that prized liquid cargo was there for the taking; within hours village residents were swarming the wreck retrieving the booze. They were off before the Coast Guard arrived.

Many a fancy yacht was sunk by the Coast Guard during a chase across the Sound. $90,000.00 worth of Chinese whiskey was found in a tunnel by police on the former Solomon Guggenheim estate in Sands Point. It seems the owner was away when the bootleggers used the estate as a hideaway. Rumor has it that Stuyvesant Fish, a man of great wealth, was awaiting the delivery of his brand new $250,000.00 yacht, when it was mistaken by the Coast Guard for another boat being sought, and machine gunned, nearly killing a young crew member. Before the boat sank, its new paneling was torn out in a search for illegal liquor goods, but nothing was ever found.

The Sound is no longer resplendent with its *"Vigilant," "Columbia," "Resolute," "Enterprise,"* J. P. Morgan's *"Corsair"* and other famous yachts of yesteryear.

Every town had its share of speakeasies: there was the Black Cat in Glen Cove, now Gerlick's Restaurant; the Graveyard Inn, hidden away behind the Hillside Cemetery; and Moldetta's, where they served their brew in porcelain tea cups. The popular retreats were raided by police one night and open for business the next.

Royal Living and Sometimes Even Royalty

It was here on the North Shore that, for the first time in American history, a foreign king, hearing of the fabled estates, came over bringing his entire fortune with him. King Zog, one-time ruler of Albania, found Knollwood in Syosset and flamboyantly paid for it with a bucket full of diamonds and rubies. Long Island's rich preferred to enjoy their showplaces tucked away in private seclusion. High ivy-covered walls, serpentine hedges, and imposing gates were all the outside world ever saw of this luxury land. Only in winter could a passing driver catch a glimpse of a castle turret or a villa whose peaked rooftop would tower above the bare trees. Entire mansions were brought from Europe stone by stone, and reconstructed atop hills overlooking the Sound. To decorate the opulent interiors, vast collections of paintings, French tapestries, oak paneled doors, ornate marble fireplaces, Oriental rugs and gilded mirrors were shipped in quantity from all parts of the world. Even the cobblestones from an historic street in Paris were brought over and reconstructed as a driveway on one estate. Surrounding the baronial homes were charming pool pavilions, indoor and outdoor tennis courts, as well as rambling stables, miles of greenhouses, tea houses, classic love temples, built-in pipe organs, polo fields and even a few private golf courses.

With the Depression of the Thirties, this area suffered some drastic changes. Many of the North Shore families survived the heavy taxation through frequent

SEAWANHAKA CORINTHIAN YACHT CLUB, WHERE FAMOUS YACHTS OF THE NORTH SHORE TYCOONS WERE MOORED.

intermarriages with each other, in the hope that their extravagant way of life could continue. Today it has become impossible to maintain the large staffs of servants needed to care for the huge homes. Even the well-to-do must closely calculate the price of extra help.

The Long Island Set

The Long Island Set, as it was known, was very much a principled world unto itself. These people lived by graceful codes of protocol, and maintained an air of decency and dignity, and if they occasionally fell from grace, the people who lived by those rules never forgot that they existed. This "set" had, and still has, its exclusive clubs, the much coveted memberships to either the Piping Rock, Creek, or Seawanhaka Corinthian Yacht Club. Lands of members of the set were always open to their neighbors who belonged to it, and riders on horseback could find their way across the North Shore through the many connecting trails. It should also be noted that the caretakers, gatekeepers, and other staff of an estate were often well taken care of. When a member of that society died it was often stipulated in the will that those who worked on an estate all their lives were allowed to remain in the often charming and rustic little estate cottages.

THE GRAND SALON OF HARBOR HILL, WHERE THE PRINCE OF WALES WAS ENTERTAINED IN 1924. *From the Donaldson Collection, Roslyn Library*

Despite the recorded extravagances and rumored wild parties, there was a quiet sense of order in this land: everyone knew his job. There were rituals and patterns that went on like clockwork; the stables had their schedules, the greenhouses still another. There were forty-room homes where the flowers were cut fresh each day and arranged in perfect order by a parlor maid. There would be one person to polish all the brass, and it was considered an honor to polish the silver—usually the butler's job. Still another of the help would iron the newspaper each day and present it to the master of the house. It was also the butler who personally called to invite the hundred or so guests three or four weeks before an upcoming dinner party. I am told that the domestic staffs on Long Island were in fact similar to the staff of the TV series "Upstairs, Downstairs," but that no American family had an all-English staff. The butler, who was head of the house, was usually English, but the footmen could be Irish, Swedish, or Scottish; the ladies' maids were often French; chambermaids and parlor maids Irish; and many of the kitchen maids were of Irish extraction.

The domestic staff system was as rigid as a steel rail; if you had domestic help you had to know the rules. Elizabeth Babcock of Woodbury remembers, "it was like running a large hotel, the business of moving all the servants, children, and all the needful things to spend a month's vacation in a rented house in Maine, the Adirondacks, or, say, Newport. It took careful planning and endless lists of all the linen, blankets, towels, silver, crystal, and china that had to be packed and sent by train so all would be ready for a dinner party thirty-six hours later. If there was a slip-up you were not forgiven."

In some cases the servants were called upon to perform odd jobs, depending on the whims and eccentricities of the master of the house. On one estate in Oyster Bay Cove, the head gamekeeper, who maintains an extensive aviary of exotic birds, ducks and wild life for conservationist Winston Guest, Jr., doubles as a chauffeur in the fall to drive the privileged ducks south for the winter rather than have them fly down like common ordinary ducks. I recall a conversation at a party during which one *grande dame* commented, "Why of course they can fly; thank God they don't *have* to."

It is said that Rudolph Valentino's ineptitude as a gardner on one of the old North Shore estates caused him to seek other means of employment and a start in the film world.

Aliza Mellon Bruce, heir to the Andrew Mellon fortune, had in addition to her villa in Woodbury, seven apartments in New York City and three other estates in New Jersey. While she only visited her sprawling Long Island house three weeks out of the year, she maintained a full domestic staff of twelve in the house and twenty-two gardeners outside, who changed the flowers each day, whether those in the thirty-two rooms had been wilted or not. Her daughter, who would have inherited the fortune, disappeared in her private plane, along with her husband, while flying over the Bermuda Triangle. No trace of them was ever found. On the Marion Brewster estate in Glen Cove, part of the routine was the spring and fall ritual in which all the silver, usually housed in a floor-to-ceiling safe in the pantry was spread out on the sixty-foot living room carpet for inventory and polishing. On still another private estate, a full-time security guard and police dog keep watch over a million-dollar, eight-foot-high bronze Renoir statue that stands watch at the edge of a secluded swimming pool.

Life could be quite lonely for the children who were raised by governesses while socialite parents hobnobbed around the world. The children were often chauffeured to private schools like Friends' Academy and the Greenvale and Eastwoods schools or sent to boarding schools, seeing their parents only during holidays. With like seeking like, the vast new fortunes huddled together, and matched each other's acquired expensive tastes. So attracted were they to the English styles and customs, they admirably set out to follow the English traditions: the horse became the root of North Shore life as it was of English country life. August Belmont, with his circle of friends, established the Meadowbrook Hunt Club in 1881, long before the first Gold Coast mansion was ever built.

Fox hunting flourished with great elegance on the North Shore; fine ladies and gentlemen in "pink" coats made a noble sight streaking across the lush green countryside at breakneck speed. Today the anise seed bag has replaced the almost extinct little fox. The trail is laid in advance by a "drag boy," and often takes a bit of tricky planning. Red jackets are still referred to as pink coats, and the Meadowbrook Toppers wore flashlight blue waistcoats. The Whips, who control the hounds, always wore black caps, and white breeches with high black boots. Few of the fifty or so riders on a hunt could keep up the frantic hill-and-dale chase to the finish.

No group has been hit harder by the shrinking of wide open cross country trails than the horsey set, that tally-hoing, fence-jumping, fox-chasing blue-blooded elite that

TEMPLETON, THE HOME OF WINSTON GUEST

often rode six days a week for six weeks straight in pursuit of voracious hounds running at a feverish pace from one estate to the next. And there were fancy hunt breakfasts and lavish balls to follow.

Polo is still very much the ultimate status symbol; once considered the best on Long Island, people came from all over the country and Europe to watch the games in Old Westbury. Old Westbury hosted a number of stars of the day, like Laddie Stanford; Winston Guest, who received a string of polo ponies as a wedding present; Stewart Inglehart; Sonny Whitney. As recalled by one of the members, "You could have a hell of a good time in the best of company, for polo was an exclusive game . . . it had an allure back in the old days, you didn't have to be the greatest athlete in the world—a good pony was the thing."

It was a time of great style, where the wealthy surrounded themselves with big cars, gorgeous clothes, lots of parties and fun. A typical day on the Gold Coast would start with a game of golf on a private course, then lunch at the Piping Rock Club terrace with much talk of horses, then on to the Meadowbrook Club where the game of polo came alive. With one's friends, one would fill the Rolls Royces and head for the nearest dinner party that often ended with a Charleston contest. But the Meadowbrook Club is no more; the Long Island Expressway and fenced-in housing developments have blocked the once-endless trails. There is still the Smithtown Hunt Club, though never referred to in the same breath by the old and much revered Meadowbrook Club members.

Long Island still remembers its great American horsemen; their portraits line the walls of the Old Guard club houses: men like Ambrose Clark, Pete Bostwick, Thomas Hitchcock, Francis P. Garvan and Jock Whitney, who owned the famous Greentree stables, in Manhasset. W. Gould Brokaw of Great Neck had his own half mile race track where he held his own races, open to local folk, complete with bookmakers. One man, C. K. G. Billings, who built Farnsworth in Oyster Bay carried his love for horses to its extreme by giving one of the most original parties on record: a white-tie-and-tails formal dinner party for thirty-six guests on horseback. Miniature tables, complete with the finest linen were attached to the pommels of the saddles; dinner was served by waiters dressed as grooms at a hunt party. Not to leave out the equine guests, fancy oat-filled feeding bags were set before each horse, and all dined in elegance together.

The Buckram Beagles, still another North Shore tradition, was founded in 1934, though the ancient sport dates back 5,000 years to the primitive peoples of Asia Minor. The landed gentry on Long Island met on Sundays in their handsome forest green jackets, white stock and slacks, and black velvet caps. At the sight of the hare, the master of the hounds would cry "Tally Ho!" sending the members hallooing and jogging across the rolling hills and woods of Old Westbury and Brookville. In its day, the Buckram Beagles was a subscription organization of about seventy families, who split the cost of maintaining the kennels and the beagle pack.

During the Second World War, the club fell on hard times and the kennels had to be sold—each member in good standing was asked to take home a beagle, depending upon the size of the home. One society matron, whose house numbered some sixty rooms, was presented with eight of the yelping, ever-sniffing creatures, who roamed about in her ballroom. I'm told that in a fit of disgust her husband threw one of them in the clothes dryer, tossing it about for a while. He hoped it would calm the poor creature down, but alas, it only came out fluffier.

There is one case on record where the famous Buckram Beagles were taken to New York's Lincoln Center, where they were to add their baying as a special effect to Mozart's "Hunting Symphony," performed by the Festival Orchestra. The beagles were to proceed in orderly fashion across the stage, and when given their cue, sing along with the music. Unfortunately, when applause broke out from the surprised concertgoers, the hounds lost control of themselves and leaped into the audience, sniffing about and running up and down the aisles. Hounds abounded at the Beagle Ball held each winter at the Piping Rock Club. It was as much a tradition as the hunt itself, though the beagles did not attend. With most of the wide-open cross country spaces dead-end affairs today, the Buckram members were forced to disband, though their love of the fresh air has them out on winter Sundays jogging about the old estates as members of the equally exclusive Wheezer Walk Club.

Another unique North Shore group is the Victorian Picnic Club, who together with the "Friends of Abandonded Gazebos," a preservation organization, meet on alternate Sundays throughout the summer months seeking out abandoned gazebos from the abandoned remaining estates. Both groups work together to restore them; once completed, they stage elegant turn-of-the-century picnics complete with the finest china, crystal, silver tea sets and linen laid out in the garden pavilions. In an effort to preserve a charming tradition, woman members are often seen wearing white organdy gowns, straw picture hats, and shielding themselves from the sun with parasols.

MARSHALL FIELD'S STABLE FOR HIS FAMOUS RACE HORSES

TERRACE AT PLANTING FIELDS, THE COE ESTATE

PLANTING FIELDS, MRS. W. R. COE'S BATHROOM IN THE 1920's

VANDERBILT ESTATE COLUMNS

The Mansions Today

The W. C. Bird estate is probably one of the most tragic and macabre of the ruined houses on the North Shore. Built in 1915 by C. K. G. Billings, a financier, it became the site of one tragedy after another. Billings built the house for his son, who died in the First World War without ever having seen it. Farnsworth, as it was known, was then bought by Wallace C. Bird for his wife Winifred. Life came to an end at Farnsworth in 1941 when Mr. Bird lost his life when his private plane went out of control and crashed not far from his home. Mrs. Bird, who wore mourning black for the rest of her life, then had the remains of the plane crated and placed in a tunnel down in the basement. From then on the house was boarded up, and never lived in again. Years passed and time took its toll, the vandals came, and senseless destruction followed. All the priceless furnishings were stolen one by one. In 1961, Mrs. Bird was murdered with an overdose of drugs by her psychiatrist, and since there were no heirs, the mansion was condemned as a liability to the property. In 1966 the fabled showplace, built to last five hundred years, succumbed to the wrecker's ball.

LAND'S END. F. SCOTT FITZGERALD IS SAID TO HAVE WRITTEN PARTS OF HIS NOVEL, *THE GREAT GATSBY*, FROM THIS PORCH OVERLOOKING LONG ISLAND SOUND AS A GUEST OF BAYARD SWOPE. HE USED IT AS THE INSPIRATION FOR THE HOME OF DAISY BUCHANNON. IT IS NOW IN PRIVATE HANDS.

The Gold Coast, though tarnished now, is still spotted with wealth and power. Some of the great mansions are still privately owned, but these are the exceptions. Hempstead House, the former home of Daniel Guggenheim, is a hundred-and-twenty-room castle. Standing high upon a cliff in Sands Point, it is now owned by Nassau County and will one day be a park. The famed Old Westbury Gardens, the former John Phipps estate, is open to the public at certain times of the year, as are the Planting Fields Arboretum in Oyster Bay, and the Vanderbilt Mansion in Centerport. A large number of other estates have been converted into schools or private country clubs that make good use of the stables, pools, and tennis courts. Tax-exempt monasteries and convents are also scattered throughout the area.

Inisfada, former home of Nicolas Brady, had all the makings of a minor kingdom. It was once considered the fourth largest home in America in 1917 and six million dollars was spent on the furnishings alone. It also had a beamed ceiling that was once part of an English castle and boasts a fifty-foot-long Persian carpet from Buckingham Palace. Today it is used by the St. Ignatius Retreat House. Beekman Towers, built by August Belmont, is the house I believe Fitzgerald described in his classic, *The Great Gatsby*. The feudal castle "was a colossal affair by any standard—it was a

F. W. WOOLWORTH ESTATE, AND THE BELVEDERE KING NEPTUNE FOUNTAIN

factual imitation of some Hotel de Ville in Normandy, with a tower on one side." That beloved American landmark is no more, but it is possible that the huge white colonial house that still stands in the grand manner across the Bay in Sands Point was the home of Daisy Buchanan, Gatsby's lost love. The long white pier and haunting green light he refers to in his book either never existed or have long since fallen into the sea.

Other mansions have vanished, and only ruins are left to mark the places where the rich once reveled. The L. C. Tiffany mansion mysteriously burned to the ground in the late 'Fifties, leaving a gaunt chimney as if standing sentinel over a blackened ruin. Close by, a huge web-like arbor begins to sag with time and the weight of vines that have not been pruned in decades. All that remains of the William D. Guthrie estate in Lattington is an empty pool surrounded by deteriorating Doric columns. A marble balustrade is a lonely reminder of where the main house once stood.

The F. W. Woolworth mansion is one of the few opulent marble palaces still maintained. Now in private hands, it is often used as a location site for films, and television commercials. The sixty-two room manor house was built in 1917 at a cost of $9,000,000, taking its inspiration from the Borghese Gardens in Rome. The driveway entrance is graced by a great panorama of marble statuary. King Neptune stands in a pool amid pink marble horses. A classic gazebo draped with wisteria sets off the formal gardens.

The inside would have dazzled Gatsby himself—from top to bottom it was built to impress. The all-marble staircase in the main hall alone cost $2,000,000. There are solid gold fixtures throughout the house. An Italian marble fireplace stands fourteen feet high in the baroque ballroom, which is set off by a fourteen karat gold gilded ceiling. A lattice-work panel slides back to reveal a massive pipe organ. The bedrooms upstairs were something to behold; each room was done in a style of a different period in time. Walking down the endless hall one passed the Marie Antoinette Room, the Napoleon Room, Ming Dynasty Room, the Edwardian Room, and one done in the style of the Louis XVI period.

Not far down the road we come to an area known by local folk as the Pratt Oval. At one time it covered a good part of Glen Cove's shoreland. Charles Pratt, who worked

THE GREAT HALL, FERGUSON CASTLE

along with Rockefeller of Standard Oil fame, eventually had eighteen estates for himself and his family. Pratt built Dasoris Park, a sixty-acre patch of private stables, a carriage house complex, and garages for their motor cars. The buildings still stand in a state of ruin; the bright orange tile and copper-topped clock tower are set way back from the main road. At one time there were twenty-two miles of bluestone roads surrounding this estate.

The most impressive of the houses was the one built by Herbert L. Pratt, which is now Webb Institute, a private school for naval architects. The former George D. Pratt home is now the Russian embassy in Glen Cove; Harrison House across the way is now a retreat for executives.

Welwyn, former home of Harold Erving Pratt, now owned by Nassau County, is being planned as a wildlife preserve, and one of the most breathtaking sights to behold on the island is the black and white pine forest that overlooks the Sound. One of the original piers is still standing at the water's edge; at one time two-hundred-foot yachts could dock there and enjoy the comforts of the rustic beach house that stood among the pine trees. Though it was struck by vandals recently and burned to the ground, the spot is still a magically haunting place to visit, with the wind blowing through the lofty branches and the incessant cries of the gulls.

Few of the Gold Coast mansions had so dramatic a setting as the home of Frances P. Garvan in Old Westbury. Set high amidst endless rolling lawns, its gabled roof and tower could be seen for miles around. It was bulldozed in 1974 and now there are forty smaller houses on the original one hundred and ten acres. The impressive Tudor mansion was crowned with a Victorian cupola, and a Gothic tower on one side. It had stood abandoned since the death of the owner in 1937. Even the sinister stone lions that stood wraith-like in the garden could not guard against its inevitable destruction.

Today stories of ghosts and scandals surround many of the great houses. There is a castle in Huntington where cries are heard from a hundred-foot tower that rises up from a cliff overlooking the Sound. A young servant is said to have jumped to his death from the tower. Legend has it that the daughter of F. W. Woolworth reappears to haunt the garden pavilion where she secretly met her lover. She died heartbroken when her father forbade her to see him again. She has been seen time and time again, always wearing the same faded blue dress. At Ferguson's Castle, rumor has it that the dining room floor was paved with tombstones from children's graves, and there are tales of an eccentric mother who had a wax dummy made of her son after he hung himself from a beam in an abandoned water tower. In nearby Old Westbury, an admirer of Mrs. Sonny Whitney jumped to his death from a twelve story water tower, after Mrs. Whitney failed to show up at the unveiling of a nude statue he had made of her. She then had the statue boarded up; it still stands forgotten in the garden.

Despite the many overtones of tragedy, there is something magical and disturbingly beautiful about the North Shore estates. Even after decades of neglect, they continue to stand in regal dignity like fantasies from another dimension in time and space, colossal ruins whose transient beauty captures the spirit of an age that will never come again.

FERGUSON CASTLE, BYZANTINE FOUNTAIN

ORMSTON HOUSE, STATUE

The Mansions

A FOUNTAIN STANDS ALONE IN KING ZOG'S
GARDEN WALL

COINDRE HALL

Coindre Hall, built in 1906 by George McKesson Brown, can best be seen from Huntington Harbor. It rises up over the water like some dream castle out of a fairy tale. The house was originally copied from two castles in the south of France, and is one of the unique manor houses to be found on the North Shore. Mr. Brown, owner of a pharmaceutical firm, spent much of his time traveling throughout Europe, collecting furnishings for his massive home. He also brought back with him nine unusual trees, each from a different country. They still stand at the front of the drive. Set between two turrets is a gabled dormer flanked by copper dolphins. The front medieval façade encloses a sun porch. The conoidal towers roofed with tile contained both the dining room and a spiral staircase made of teak wood. A spacious entrance hall with terra cotta tiled floor contains a huge grandfather clock, the only remaining original piece of furniture in the house today.

The manor, one of the first to be built on the North Shore, was equipped with central heating, unusual for that time. In summer the house was air cooled with ice that had been gathered from the lake and stored in an ice house. There was also a sauna bath and a fifteen-foot indoor pool on the first floor. At the far end of a sweeping lawn was a private dock on the water and a boat house, which once housed a massive yacht. In its day the boat house, a miniature replica of the main house, was decorated with trophies and nautical equipment. The gardens surrounding the estate were kept very simple; well manicured lawns stretching miles down to the beach held a breathtaking view from the rear veranda. Coindre Hall saw much quiet and dignified entertaining until 1940, when it was sold to a Catholic order. It is presently being used by the Suffolk County Park Commission.

Mr. Brown and his wife remained on the estate for some time after the house was sold, and lived in the servants' quarters. The castle is best known for its awesome looking water tower, which is visible for miles. The tower, with peaked roof reminiscent of feudal times, is now a roosting place for thousands of blackbirds who gather there atop the roof's rotting timbers.

THE MEDIEVAL WATER TOWER

FRONT FAÇADE

COINDRE HALL

THE BOAT HOUSE

GARVAN FROM THE AIR

GARVAN ESTATE

There was only one way to experience the Garvan estate, and that was from a small low-flying plane. The day I flew over it, as luck would have it, there was a fox hunt riding through. It was a clear crisp fall day, and the trees were a blaze of color as the tiny white-tipped sterns of the hounds could barely be seen as they scattered across the fields below, past the great Tudor manor house. It was one of the last hunts to come through this way. The sound of plane's engine made it impossible to hear the all-familiar subtle sounds of the hunt, but somehow in my head I could hear the thundering hooves and wail of the huntsman's horn despite the noise.

Francis P. Garvan, who was president of the Chemical Foundation, Inc. built the sixty-room English Tudor mansion in 1891 just before it became popular to build in the area.

Eclectic in style, the house was set off with a magnificent copper Victorian cupola. There were Gothic gables and a bright-colored Spanish tiled roof that was so heavy that over the years the entire house began to sag from the weight of it. In the center of the circular drive stood an ornate marble wishing well surrounded by clipped boxwood hedges. Just over the front door was a carved frieze with the date 1891 surrounded by a scroll pattern. High above it on either side were two platforms, each supporting a carved statue of the Renaissance period. Inside the spacious hall there stood a broad and sweeping staircase with a wide leaded glass window at the mid-way landing. All the ceilings throughout the main floor were like wedding cake, all white plaster filigree done by European artists.

A beautiful hand-hewn oak paneled chapel stood at the far east wing of the house. In the library there were richly decorated leaded glass windows with stained glass insets imported from Europe. All about the room were stacks of dust-covered books with titles like *Fluffs Guide to Turf—1930*, and *Foxhunting Formalities*, with odd messages like "always refer to your beagles as hounds, please." The house had not been lived in since Garvan's death in 1937, and most of the handsome furnishings had been removed over the years by the family, though in one of the rooms on the third floor there was a charming Louis XVI chaise longue standing in a lonely corner of the room. The second and third floors were most interesting to explore; mold covered the large steamer trunks, and boxes lay on the floors and in the hallways. Judging from the dates on the newspapers, they were packed in 1944. In one of the closets, old discolored white organdy gowns hung on rusty hangers, and nearby there were several hat boxes containing straw picture hats with faded pink and blue silk flowers hanging from them.

In a dark corner of the attic was a large black leather trunk with the gold initials F.P.G. on it; inside, lovingly packed away, were beautiful old tweed riding jackets and well-worn Bedford cord breeches, and a pair of fine English boots that knew their days of glory on many a hill-and-dale chase. The floors were badly warped and at odd angles; they creaked as you walked on them and felt as though they would collapse at any moment. Outside, huge marble lions guarded the entrance to the garden that was

FAÇADE FACING THE SOUTH LAWN

surrounded by a balustraded and ivy-covered brick wall. One of the charming features was a colorful Madonna and child ceramic sculpture fashioned after Della Robbia.

STABLES

HAND CARVED OAK PANELING IN THE LIBRARY

A SIXTEENTH CENTURY WOODEN STATUE OVER MAIN ENTRANCE DOOR

A DELLA ROBBIA IN THE GARDEN WALL

HALF TIMBER DETAIL THROUGH THE WROUGHT IRON OF THE WISHING WELL

On either side of the garden stood a terra cotta tiled and timbered gazebo, where the Garvan children had played and had been told stories by their English nannies. Now the graceful form of the gazebos was obscured by the masses of untended vines. There was a time when horses could gallop through the stately arcade of stone arches, now buried by brambles and ivy.

Also found on the 101-acre estate is a handsome rambling stable. Now only a handful of horses remain, with their eighty-year-old trainer Edward Fitzpatrick, who has worked there most of his life. At one end of the stable there is a wood paneled trophy room, filled with mementoes of grander days; one wall is covered with hundreds of dust-covered red, yellow, and blue ribbons. A stuffed fox head with glaring eyes hangs over the door.

The saddest thing for me was to return several years later, and arrive just as the towering cupola fell to the ground. Now there was the agonizing drone of the bulldozer doing violence to our past. Still, all I could hear was the thundering hooves and the huntmaster's trumpet signal to hurry to the chase—for one last time.

AERIAL VIEW FROM THE SOUTH

PEMBROKE

It is often said that people use their homes as stages and playgrounds. This is certainly true of Captain De Lamar whose accomplishments seem almost fictional in our present day. His enormous wealth and imagination led him to build Pembroke, a 1914 manor house of the most titanic proportions. Legend has it that Capt. De Lamar was found by sailors in the waters of the Mediterranean and was so named De Lamar, Italian for "from the sea." He spent his early days on board ships, and after visiting all the ports in the world, he came to America as a contractor. He made millions salvaging old sunken ships, and when gold fever struck in Leadville in 1878, he invested in claims, making still more millions.

A man of endless talents and abilities, he then entered politics and became state senator of Idaho. In his spare time he was president of Dome Mines, vice-president of

Delta Sugar Co., International Nickel Co, and American Bank Note Co. Though a quiet man by nature, the lavish parties that he gave at Pembroke in Glen Cove became legendary. He often entertained guests by showing silent movies in his private theater, whose walls were painted with colorful murals depicting well-known scenes from "The Sheik," westerns of the day, and Charlie Chaplin films. He often had the film stars themselves attend his gala costume balls that went on for days.

Grandeur, originality, and theatrical flair distinguished De Lamar's neo-classic styled home; a vast collection of rare palms and colorful tropical plants were housed in a mammoth glass palm house, which covered almost an acre in size. Designed as a horticultural museum, its palm trees towered some thirty-five feet amid the luxuriant flowering foliage. At the far end of the room was a curious, almost sinister-looking cave, or grotto, encrusted with stalactites that gave it the appearance of sharpened teeth through a wide open mouth. A statue of a nude woman stood in the shallow water and was reflected in a mirror set deep in the cave. At one time water cascaded down its rocky surface and flowed into a stream that wound its way through all parts of the room. Numerous vividly colored tropical birds flew about, adding their song to the sounds of rippling water. There were two ornate metal bridges so one could cross from one wing to the other.

In the center of the main section, where the room towered up some sixty feet at its highest point, there was a large round tiled swimming pool. A gazebo or pavilion made of ornamental metal work and Tiffany-style glass stood on a rise in the center of the pool. Directly over it was a circular gallery with a metal railing from where guests could dive into the pool below. In an adjoining wing that branched out from the main court was the orangerie where tropical fruit, oranges, grapefruit, and bananas were grown. Off in one corner was a staircase that led down to the moving picture gallery

INDOOR POOL WITH THE CAVE IN THE BACKGROUND

THE END OF AN ERA, GUEST WING

THE PALM COURT. WATERFALL AND CAVE

with its plush red velvet and gold fringed draperies. There were also a squash court, bowling alley and shooting range for the pleasure of guests. In another section were the heating units and other mechanical equipment and storerooms. A huge tank and pump kept the water circulating in the streams and waterfalls above. An elaborate electrical

PEMBROKE. FAÇADE FACING THE SOUND

CAPTAIN DELAMAR'S PRIVATE STONE PIER

system was designed to illuminate the palm house and pool at night. From the Sound it shone like a blazing diamond against the sky.

One entered the eighty-room manor house through a marble vestibule. On either side was a niche—each containing a classic statue, lit from the back. The main hall was reminiscent of the grand old movie palaces built around the turn of the century. A large French Renaissance mantel dominated one wall and on the landing of the broad and spacious staircase was a pipe organ hidden behind an elaborate fretwork panel. All the rooms on the main floor were large and laid out for entertaining hundreds of guests. There was a paneled billiard room with ornamental cornices and parquet floors, and a French Renaissance reception room provided a wonderful view of the Sound and the boathouse that stood at the water's edge. There were also a den, dining room, powder room, and breakfast room with mirrored walls set behind a latticework frame. An unusual leaded glass ceiling filled the room with light, while wide picture windows allowed a view of the gardens. The rear loggia ran almost the entire length of the west wing and was filled with gay summer wicker furniture; potted ferns stood on marble pedestals.

Throughout the house were pleasant surprises. Even on the roof, there was a sun parlor or pergola surrounded by a colorfully planted roof garden. Before Pembroke was completed, De Lamar died in 1918 at the age of seventy-five, after an operation. The house was closed for some time after his death, and was eventually bought by Arthur Loew of movie theatre fame. It enjoyed a second heyday of parties and lavish social gatherings. In the 'Fifties it was again closed up, for the last time. No one had lived in the main house for some fifteen years by the time it was bulldozed in 1968. Unlike most other abandoned houses, it had been safe from vandals up to that time: the owner had ordered the downstairs windows and doors to be sealed up in cement for reasons unknown. Only the pale lavender glass from the palm court had been shattered by storms over the years.

When I first saw the place back in the early 'Sixties,—even as a ruin it was still breathtaking—the towering palms had slumped over from lack of water, no water flowed from the grotto, and the statue was gone. No one knows what had become of the metal and glass gazebo that once stood in the center of the pool. When the bulldozers came, the huge green glass Tiffany globe with two lavender butterflies on it was still hanging some thirty feet above the cave from a heavy iron chain. It seemed no one could figure a way to get it down. I couldn't bear to watch it shatter along with the rest of this doomed paradise.

Today all that remain of Pembroke are the skeletal frames of the greenhouses and the outbuildings, indoor tennis court, garages and a ten story water tower enshrouded in ivy. One can still make out what was once a beautiful Japanese garden with reflecting ponds, connected by lacy wrought iron bridges. A winding stone colonnade and terra cotta tiled tea house, flanked by marble statuary, stands solemnly in the entrance garden. For many years Pembroke stood out like some fantasy from another dimension in time. It is sadder still that but for a few, no one ever saw past the massive iron gates that guarded the entrance. Even as a ruin its beauty captured the spirit of the Gatsby age.

LOGGIA

SOUTH PORTICO.

WATER TOWER AND STABLES
IN THE BACKGROUND

REAR VIEW OF THE HOUSE THROUGH THE GARDEN PAVILION

WINFIELD

F. W. Woolworth

Winfield today is still the grandest of the grand North Shore palaces. It is also the only marble manor house still standing. It has survived storms, leaks, taxes, vandals, suicide, scandal, screaming ghosts, X-rated movies, police raids, and even one account of a UFO landing on the roof. It is a house that would have dazzled Gatsby himself. From top to bottom it was built to impress.

WINFIELD. THE TWO MILLION DOLLAR STAIRWAY

Woolworth started out on $3.50 a week as a clerk, but his mother is said to have told him as a child, "Some day, my son, you will be a rich man." It turned out to be an understatement. Woolworth was twenty-seven when he opened his first five-and-ten cent dry goods store in Lancaster, Pennsylvania on a $300 loan. On opening day he masterminded the idea of branch stores. Perhaps to fulfill his mother's prophecy, he drove himself to near collapse from overwork. It wasn't long before he amassed his millions and was caught in the spirit of one-upmanship, as was the trend of the day. To gain the attention of one's peers, one had to build the biggest yacht, race the fastest horse, own the tallest building, live in the most grandiose house, and fill it with hand-me-downs from royalty. Woolworth was proud to say he slept in Napoleon's bed and that Mrs. Woolworth did her hair at the dressing table that Marie Antoinette once used.

Entering the skyscraper competition, Woolworth managed to build the tallest building in the world, paying for it with thirteen million dollars in cash. Having done this, his next venture was to build a marble palace on the North Shore. The Woolworths had been living on a sprawling water view estate in Glen Cove that he had bought from Emmet Queens around the turn of the century. In 1916 a tragic fire all but destroyed the Mediterranean stucco mansion, along with a valuable collection of Persian rugs and paintings. Woolworth had his marble palace built on the remaining charred foundation, though only the West façade pillars, sleeping porch, and solarium bore any resemblance to the original house. In 1916 he commissioned architect Charles P. H. Gilbert to design one of the most opulent homes built during the Gold Coast era, at an estimated cost of $9,000,000. A mile-long circular driveway takes the driver past a wide panorama of marble Roman statuary, King Neptune stands in a pool amid pink marble horses, and on the north side of the house, the formal gardens are patterned after the Borghese gardens in Rome. At one time 24 gardeners worked full time to maintain the Long Island showplace. Two limestone gazebos draped in wisteria in spring stand on either side of the garden. In the center an enchanting fountain, outlined with a stone balustrade, features a statue of a boy holding a dolphin. From its mouth water rises 12 feet into the air. On the other side of the pool, a classic summer pavilion, with open loggia of arched pillars, is flanked by an arched wrought iron arbor.

The west wing is perhaps the most impressive, with four enormous pillars soaring up to the third floor from the balustraded veranda. Colorful ceramic tiles cover the terrace floor. The wing overlooks a staircase with wide steps that lead down to a circular terrace with a round marble fountain. Another flight of stairs ascends to an alley of linden trees, lining a path that is terminated by an iron gate.

A large stone building with a bell tower was once the carriage house. It overlooks the greenhouses that are now in a state of advanced decay. Vandals have broken all of the glass and the steel structure is almost lost beneath a tangle of savage vines. There are also a swimming pool and tennis court, though they were added by the last owners. Inside the 56-room Italian Renaissance manor, the grand staircase is one of the most costly ever built—an estimated $2,000,000. Though basically simple in design, the pink and beige polished marble adds a warm tone to the otherwise austere foyer. The

AERIAL VIEW OF WINFIELD

original brass light fixture still hangs from the ornamental plaster coffered ceiling trimmed in blue and 14K gold leaf.

To the right of the hall is an 18th century Georgian dining salon. Paneled walls are graced by elaborate carving in limestone wood after the manner of the famous 18th century carver Grinling Gibbons. The lighting sconces dotting the walls and two huge chandeliers are sterling silver. To the far end of the room, though separated by a bronze grillwork, is an all-glass solarium or palm court with an enchanting marble fountain set against a treillaged wall. Though empty now, the room was once filled with French wicker furniture covered in delicate floral patterned fabric and surrounded by palms, hydrangeas and Boston ferns.

MAIN ENTRANCE

Everything about the house was spendidly decorated. The arrangement of the rooms followed a variety of moods and pleasant changes. Off to the right of the dining room is a mahogany paneled billiard room, and to the left of it were the vast kitchens and pantries, where a tremendous walk-in refrigerator was used to store food for hundreds of guests. The kitchen cooking stove is twenty feet long, and a ten-foot walk-in safe was used to store the silver. Just to the left of the center hall Woolworth had a private study, in the French Gothic style with walnut woodwork trimmed with deep green damask fabric, where he spent much of his time.

Woolworth's reign here was short lived. He died only two years after the house was completed, of septic poisoning after he refused to seek the help of a dentist. The house was then closed up for many years and then bought in 1929 by Mrs. Richard S. Reynolds of Reynolds Metal Co. I was about fourteen when I first saw this magical place. I remember it as though it were yesterday. No one was around, and though it was not by any means abandoned it had the feeling of not being used. I remember it was late in the day and the west wing was flushed with gold, catching the last rays of sunlight. I had

come in from the rear gate where the trees resemble a cathedral nave. From the bottom of those great stairs the house rose up like some majestic phantom lost in time. Without giving any thought as to why I was there, I walked up to the veranda, looked in through the French doors, and caught my first glimpse of what was indeed the most dazzling room I had ever seen. It was truly a ballroom of classic grandeur with a crystal and gold chandelier that was about seven feet across. Its high vaulted ceiling was encrusted with 14 karat gold, harp-bearing cherubs engaged in flight. One wall was dominated by a 16-foot Italian marble fireplace decorated with angels and mythological beasts.

It was many years later that I met the owner who followed the Woolworths' reign, Mrs. Reynolds. A charming anachronism from a time of grander ways, she was as vibrant as her bright red hair. As she talked nostalgically about the past, it became apparent that she'd lost some portion of her life forever and still thought as though it were the 'Twenties. "I give the most divine parties here," she said, "though I do wish Prohibition would end." With a graceful wave of her hand she excused herself, sat down

NORTH FACADE FACING THE FORMAL ROSE GARDEN AND LONG ISLAND SOUND

in front of the console of the pipe organ and ran her fingers across the keyboard, but no sound came out. I found out later that it had not worked for years. She took great pride in showing the house and reminiscing about its history. As she stood before the imposing fireplace in the entrance hall, she pointed up to the marble coat of arms Woolworth had designed when he built the house. "That's Woolworth up there on top, and the poor creature below him is his wife in the iron helmet that covers her face. She was a bit dotty, they say, and never left her room. The three girls below were of course his daughters—Jessy, Edna, and Helena.

Do you see the crack running through the second girl? They say she took her life, and on the night it happened Woolworth was giving a party for his friends. Out of nowhere a bolt of lightning struck the mantel and caused it to crack. It wasn't until the next day that they found poor Edna dead in her bed."

Woolworth loved the grand display and was fond of giving his guests the tour of the centuries. The upstairs bedrooms were something to behold: you had a choice of climbing the marble stairs or using one of two private electric elevators. The one to the

BORGHESE GARDENS

right of Woolworth's study was carved Regency walnut with gilt mirrors and a glass ceiling. Each of the main bedroom suites was done in a different period in history. Woolworth's image of himself was reflected in his private suite; it was a replica of Napoleon's palace in Compeigne, France. He had taken a fancy to the original on one of his trips abroad. His Empire-style bed was said to have once belonged to Napoleon himself. Over it was a gilt carved circular canopy with gold embroidered red velvet hanging draperies. The walls of his bath were imported pink marble, the closet doors mirrored and framed by marble pilasters. Solid gold fixtures adorn the bathtub that was cut from a solid block of Siena marble.

A simple hall, with brass lanterns providing the only decoration, runs from one end of the second floor to the other. It gives the impression of a hotel rather than a home. Yet the rooms are unique inside: there are several done in the French style; the Louis XV room; a Renaissance room; French Gothic; the Edwardian room with its ribbed and vaulted pointed decorated arches. Just to the left of the top of the stairs is the Chinese room and next to it the Ming Dynasty room, whose main feature is an 18th century Chinoiserie lacquer mantel and matching door panels. The ceiling is covered in 14K gold.

The music room would become engulfed in total darkness as the romantic symphonies began to unfold. It would gradually become light, lit with beams of colored

THE MAIN ENTRANCE HALL

THE DINING ROOM WITH THE ORIGINAL FURNITURE

lights ranging from amber, blue to mauve, varying and changing with the sweeping
tones of the music. With the changing of the compositions a life size portrait of the
composer would slowly rise up from the darkness. In the Woolworth English Gothic
Room, encircling the stone mantel is an allegorical representation of Woolworth's life.
Supporting the stone structure on either side are a woman and man, representing
Woolworth's parents. The right panel depicts him as a child, then shows him leaving his
parent's farm as a poor boy. A series of reliefs follows showing his marriage to Jennie
Creighton and the birth of his three daughters, and their own marriages. Mrs. Reynolds
related the strange coincidence concerning the death of one of the daughters.

The room that attracts the most attention is the Marie Antoinette room, which is
always kept locked. After Mrs. Reynolds moved out, during the time when the building
was used as a girls' school, there were at least thirty accounts of people who claim to have
heard a woman crying in that room. Others say they have seen a young woman, always
wearing the same faded blue dress, walking in the garden. The legend is that
Woolworth's second daughter took her own life in that room when her father forbade
her to marry the man she loved.

The present caretaker swears he communicates with an undentified creature who
taps messages to him on the basement pipes. And I remember a story one of the
secretaries told me when she was working for the school: she had spent the night in that

THE MILLION DOLLAR BALLROOM

FIREPLACE DETAIL AND GOLD CEILING IN THE MUSIC ROOM

room having no other room to go to, and was awakened by a woman crying in front of the fireplace, saying that the secretary would be joining her soon. I disregarded the story at the time, but two months later the woman was dead of heart failure.

In 1975 the Downs School, which had occupied the building since 1962, closed down and the house was put up for sale at public auction. With the taxes being nearly $60,000 a year, there were no bids on the property. All of the antiques and art were auctioned off, leaving Winfield looking like a great hollow mausoleum. But as fate would have it, it did not go the way of its doomed predecessors. It was bought a few months later by Martin Carey, the youngest brother of Governor Carey of New York, and Richard Markoll, who owns a construction company in Europe. They had met for the first time at the auction and discovered that they both loved to sing opera. Martin Carey had performed at Carnegie Hall and Mr. Markoll had sung in the bathtub, having studied opera abroad. They formed a partnership and bought Winfield together, because of the perfect acoustics of the music room. They are often heard singing into the wee hours of the morning.

After they worked for six months painstakingly restoring the mansion, the place began to come alive. The owners lent the estate as the site of the month-long 1977 Decorator Showcase, a fund-raising event where top decorators each take a room and interpret to their fancy. On the night of the grand opening, a candlelight ball was staged

F. W. WOOLWORTH'S EMPIRE BEDROOM

MAIN ENTRANCE BRONZE DOOR

at the manor. A horse and carriage transported guests from the main gate to the manor house, and later in the evening on to Welwyn, the neighboring former Pratt estate, where the dining and dancing were held under a huge pink tent. Several other private parties have been given at Winfield by the new and proud owners. Rather than use the dining room, Mr. Markoll prefers to set up a long table in front of a blazing fire in the music room. At one I attended, when he ran out of firewood, the colorful Mr. Markoll flamboyantly hurled the dining room chairs into the flames, rather than have his guests

THE ORIGINAL WEST LOGGIA DESTROYED IN THE 1916 FIRE

MRS. WOOLWORTH'S SITTING ROOM

GUEST ROOM, REDECORATED BY THE AUTHOR 1978

suffer a chill. It was truly an old guard Gold Coast gesture.

There have been other formal balls held at Winfield since the new owners came. One was given by a foreign princess "To Save Our Threatened Whales." Still another, a

A VINTAGE CAR AT THE PORTE COCHERE

fund-raising event called Monte Carlo Night, turned sour when a threatened police raid forced the gambling part of the evening to be called off. Other rumors abound. One story is that an X-rated movie was filmed there in 1975, another is that a suit ensued when an over-curious neighbor fell out of a tree while trying to check out the activities.

There were so many rumors and stories about the place that it would take an entire book to document them all. I vowed to spend the summer there, investigating as

much as I could with the help of trained parapsychologists, and arranged to spend the night there alone in order to satisfy my own curiosity about the ghosts. Armed with a tape recorder, camera, infra-red film, a timing device and two candles I placed on the mantel, I waited and hoped something would happen. The door to the Marie Antoinette room is adorned with a gold swan-shaped doornob. Having been given the key, I opened it.

There was a stillness in that room, one of quiet grieving, and unless my imagination was affected by all the stories that I'd heard, the room felt colder than the other rooms upstairs. There was a mysterious appeal about the place, despite the absence of furnishings. In the dark, the draperies on the windows looked like mourning gowns. Outside, the garden was lost beneath a blanket of heavy snow, and only the tops of the statues peeked out from under it. Inside, all along the walls were intricate plaster work panels creating the effect of a white wedding cake. French grisaille murals of robust cherubs entwined in garlands of roses in panels over the doors added a sensual note to the room, and wisps of cobwebs obscured the tiny glass crystal pendants that hung from the chandelier.

I waited all night for gray haunted things to appear in the shadows, but aside from a tapping noise on the pipes, which is hardly uncommon in old houses, nothing dramatic happened—save the moon casting a weird ethereal light on the brooding stone angels that support the mantel.

THE HAUNTED MARIE ANTOINETTE BEDROOM

THE SOLARIUM

F. W. WOOLWORTH'S STUDY

MAIN STAIRWAY, THE ROTUNDA

KNOLE

Nestled in the wooded hills of Old Westbury, behind an imposing gate is Knole, built in 1902. The former home of the late Bradley Martin was originally built for Herman B. Duryea, and is reminiscent of an Italian villa. A wide circular gravel drive leads to the simple front of the classic manor house. Heavy wooden doors with bronze lion heads stand at each side of the house. As you enter, you have the feeling that here is truly the domain of an aristocrat.

Inside a rotunda of such proportion and scale as to dwarf even the most oversized furnishings, a marble stairway swirls down into the center to join a highly polished terra cotta tile floor. On each side of the stairway, and at opposite sides of the

THE SOUTH GARDENS

room are four huge blue and white Ming vases containing rare orchids. Rising up from the great hall are three levels, the first leading off to an elaborate paneled library, and a French mirrored and floral painted drawing room. Another is an oak paneled dining room, and a living room contains many rare works of art, and antiques from France. Everywhere are huge fifteen-foot arched glass doors leading to vast formal gardens.

The second level is set off by a fireplace complemented by a pair of stuffed peacocks. The master bedroom and guest rooms extend the length of a lofty columned hall; more guest rooms and servants' quarters that appear to have been unentered in years are found on the third floor. Outside, a marble pavilion of Corinthian columns and classical statuary stands at the far end of one garden. The lower formal gardens lead off from the south terrace, with ornate iron railings, and walks are laid out as

AN ORIGINAL GUEST BEDROOM (1916)

KNOLE. AT LAWN PARTIES MUSICIANS WOULD PERFORM BEFORE THESE MARBLE COLUMNS

replicas of those found in castles in Europe. The site presents one of the most seductively beautiful scenes found on Long Island.

To the rear of the manor house is still another garden with a recently renovated reflecting pool. Originally treillage designed in the Le Notre style surrounded the entire

MANTLE IN UPSTAIRS BEDROOM

A MING VASE NEAR STAIRWAY

KNOLE. EAST FACADE

back of the garden; though the wood did not survive the years, wooded glades of dogwood and oaks still present a pleasant view from the house. The estate is now in private hands.

FORMAL GARDENS

AN IMPORTED SIXTEENTH CENTURY FAÇADE

THE CHIMNEYS

Christian Holmes Estate

Few adaptations of sixteenth century English Tudor have been as successfully represented in this country as the former home of Mrs. Christian Holmes. The great English manor house is so well suited to the gently rolling, tree-clad setting of Sands Point. The rambling forty-four-room house was built in 1930, and followed no rigid plan. It is one of the most picturesque of residences, with many varied angles, composed of a variety of interesting architectural units that form an informal whole. The romantic home is set off by leaded casements in stone-mullioned windows, changing hues of rustic stucco, and ancient ridges of irregular hand-hewn timbers. The architectural features of the rooms are as interesting and as varied as those of the exterior. Mrs. Holmes spent many years abroad collecting entire rooms with timbered ceilings, slate, and stone tiled floors. Carved ancient fireplaces were brought from different countries. The unique feature of the house is the main stairway, designed around a massive ship's mast supporting the spiral stairway. It was taken from a ship originally built in 1772.

Built at a cost of over three million dollars, the house was complete with air conditioning, a central vacuum system, and built-in fire hose system. The main hall reflects the flavor of a medieval dining hall; dark carved Jacobean oak is displayed against pale rough plaster walls, and stained glass medallions are set in the windows. A costly pipe organ was incorporated in the wall's structures. The original furniture was also of dark woods and many ancient tapestries adorned the walls.

The basement of the house was one of the first to be utilized for recreation. The rooms were complete with a bowling alley, steam baths and mirrored dressing rooms. Colorful exotic hand painted murals of tropical jungle scenes cover the walls of the lime green tiled heated swimming pool. Outside, the gardens are simple, with a rustic stone wall surrounding a rock garden and mosaic tiled pool. Evergreens enclose an artificial lake filled with swans. In the mid-'Fifties the forty-acre estate was sold for a fraction of its original cost and is now used as the Sands Point Jewish Community Center.

POOL HOUSE FIREPLACE WITH ITS 16TH CENTURY CREST

THE 16TH CENTURY FAÇADE WAS IMPORTED FROM ENGLAND

KNOLE. THE GARDNER'S COTTAGE

THE WEST LOGGIA

THE MAIN ENTRANCE GATE FROM CARSHALTON PARK, BERKSHIRE, ENGLAND

PLANTING FIELDS

The Coe Estate

The William Robertson Coe estate, known as Planting Fields, was so named for its magnificent plantings and sumptuous landscaping. Located in Oyster Bay, it is visited by many throughout the year who come to see the rare trees. Several are recorded by the Long Island Horticultural Society as being the largest of their species on Long Island. The great manor house can be seen from magnificent lawns spotted with huge linden and beech trees. An avenue of Japanese cherry trees shed a blanket of pink blossoms on the lawn in spring and the sprawling glass camellia house is a blaze of color

THE FORMAL GARDENS

all year around. The peace and beauty of this dream-like place defy description.

The seventy-six-room mansion designed by Walker and Gillette was completed in 1921 and is of Elizabethan style. It is constructed of mixed limestone laid in very much the same way as the old feudal castles in Scotland. All through the house the details are Tudor, with a touch of Norman influence. One charming exception is the soft green oval room just off the main hall, which is done in the Louis XVI style. The woodwork in the great hall and in many of the rooms is handwrought English oak.

Huge fireplaces taken from faraway castles set off the rooms; everywhere there are leaded stained glass windows made in England. Tapestries hang from the soft fawn-colored, trowelled plaster walls, along with rows of stuffed antelope, deer, and moose heads. The entrance hall is rich in character, with its tall ceiling and broad arched stone openings; the tower-like windows enhance dark hewn timbers. Heavy Gothic furnishings are dwarfed to proportion, giving the room a proper scale.

The atmosphere of the main living room was so authentic one had the feeling the room had been there for centuries. It was filled with cut velvets from Genoá, needlepoint upholstery, William and Mary chairs, Elizabethan tables, and colorful Persian rugs. On either side of the carved oak doorway hung a Van Dyck painting. They were originally from a collection once belonging to Marquis Coetanir of Genoa. One unique feature of the room is a Gothic balcony that extends out from the upper level of an adjoining room. The dining hall windows hold stained glass brought from Hever Castle in England, home of Ann Boleyn. The room was handsomely set off by a

THE SOUTH LAWN

Hispano Maresque rug and red brocade draperies. The famous Carshalton Gate, made in England in 1712, once stood at the entrance to Carshalton Park in Berkshire. The gate was bought by Coe in 1919 and now stands at the stately entrance to the estate.

THE DINING ROOM

PLANTING FIELDS

THE GREAT HALL

THE GREEN HOUSE

ENTRANCE COURT

POOL, CABANAS AND TEA HOUSE

WOODWARD ESTATE

There are those homes that might have long since been forgotten except for the bizarre events that took place in them. The Playhouse, as it was called, was just such an example. While most North Shore estates can still boast of having at least one tennis court, a pool, or stables, there are only a handful of playhouses, which are best spotted from the air because of their glowing blue glass roofs.

They are huge structures, usually separate from the main house, their walls big enough to contain the standard one-hundred-and-thirty-six-foot-long clay tennis court, and fifty-two-foot ceiling. Adjoining wings would house the steam rooms, often a pool, gym, and a number of rooms for entertaining, and guest quarters. Perhaps the most charming of these was the William Woodward playhouse in Oyster Bay Cove, originally built in 1927 by Mrs. E. F. McCann, who was the daughter of F. W. Woolworth. Set far back from the main entrance gate, it is built into an angle surrounding an L-shaped structure which houses the court. While the soft blue glass ceiling is ideal for daytime playing, there is also indirect lighting for the evening. Inside, there is a lounge whose walls are decorated with imported French paneling; at one end of the room is a balcony where guests may watch the games.

As one might guess from the mountainous size of the building, the most imposing room in the house, and at the same time the largest room ever built on the North Shore, is the great music hall, with its lofty beamed fifty-foot ceiling, a replica of a medieval dining hall. Even the huge marble fireplace recalls those found in feudal castles. One might almost expect to hear the clanking of armored guardsmen at any moment. At one time Rembrandts, rare tapestries, and medieval armorials decorated the rich oak paneled walls, while imported stained glass windows allowed the room to fill with sunlight. Oak paneling came from Castle of the Duke of Essex in Scotland. There were also two paintings by Van Dyck, including one of Lady Baltimore that hung over the massive fireplace. A Rembrandt painting hung on the East Wall. An ornately carved wood balcony at the rear of the room supported the pipe organ, which when played could be heard for miles around. Adjoining the court are several charming guest rooms, and servants' quarters.

Outside, surrounding the house, are the formal gardens, still the pride of the Woodward house. The rose garden, graced with marble statues, is flanked by lavish soft blue French treillage—reflected in twin lily pools. Stretching south of the garden, which was once maintained by twenty-two gardeners, is a magnificent allee of pines and cherry trees terminated by a marble love temple. In spring the Japanese cherry trees would bloom along that perfect path. The slightest breeze would fill the allee with clouds of

FORMAL GARDEN LEADING TO THE BALLROOM

delicate petals that would flutter about like swirls of pink snow. It was here that Helena McCann was married at one of the North Shore's most memorable weddings. To the east, at the end of a grove of pines, there was a swimming pool, now in ruins, as is the brick and flagstone tea house and cabaña that overlooked the outdoor tennis court.

The property was later bought in the 'Forties by millionaire sportsman William Woodward. His wife was the owner of America's top ranking horse Nashua. In 1955 The Playhouse became the scene of one of the most publicized tragedies in American history. On the night of October 29, Mrs. Ann Woodward, hearing a sound, and believing it to be a prowler, grabbed a British double barrel shotgun, opened the door of her bedroom to the darkened hall, and fired two shotgun blasts at close range at a shadowy figure. The blast all but removed the head of the man, who turned out to be her husband.

The Woodwards had attended a society party that same evening at Mrs. George F. Baker's estate nearby; they had talked about a prowler who had broken into the poolhouse the night before. Some of the guests were said to have overheard the Woodwards arguing just before leaving the party around midnight. There are those who shall remain nameless who believe that there was an elaborate cover-up of the tragedy. Mrs. Woodward herself is said to have committed suicide in 1976, after a book

GUEST BEDROOM DECORATED BY THE AUTHOR. WITH DECORATIVE PANEL BENEATH CANOPY TAKEN FROM THE W. C. BIRD ESTATE, AND FURNITURE FROM WINFIELD

written by a popular author disclosed some little known details about the case.

Marked by tragedy, the house was eventually closed; protected only by the dark dense forest, it became prey to vandals. Doomed to be bulldozed, it finally caught the eye of a buyer in 1966. I moved into the house with the new owners, believing it to be an ideal place to do research, and they were happy to have an extra helping hand as they set about to restore the former showplace. It was now austere to the point of severity, since most of the rich paneling had been gutted out, and was now being stored in a

DRAWING ROOM OVERLOOKING INDOOR TENNIS COURT

warehouse at nearby C. W. Post College. Somehow the place had managed to retain a certain magic, though it was an eerie place to be alone.

One sound I could never describe came from the stucco and glass indoor tennis court. Some of the window panes had been broken during a storm, and wandering black starlings would get trapped inside. Unable to find their way out again, their aimless shrieking would echo morbidly through the walls until they would eventually fall to their deaths from exhaustion.

Another curious feature of the house was that the pipe organ would play by itself, despite the fact that its main section and towering pipe structure had long since been removed. Doors would open and close by themselves. A heavy breathing sound was often heard from the lower level of the house; it would stop when one would try to investigate its origin. The house was a problem to heat in winter, and things were always breaking down. Workmen would refuse to go inside, believing it would bring them bad luck. For all its beauty, this was not a happy place to live. Today the house is empty again, and a procession of stately pines draped in ivy stands in hushed silence as though keeping watch over this seemingly haunted place.

THE SOUTH GATE FROM THE GREAT LAWN

OLD WESTBURY GARDENS

The former estate of Mr. and Mrs. John S. Phipps, now known as Old Westbury Gardens, is considered one of the showplaces on the East Coast. The Georgian manor was designed by the London architect George Crawley in 1909. The gate entrance to the estate is perhaps one of the most impressive on the North Shore. Beautiful beech and linden trees line the mile-long drive that leads to the stately manor house. The interiors of the home are furnished today as though the family were still living there; fresh flowers are brought in each day from the greenhouses. Most of the furnishings are of the Georgian period, and are complemented by a number of paintings by Sir Joshua Reynolds, Sir Henry Raeburn, Gainsborough, and John Singer Sargent. The lavish rooms are decorated with gilded mirrors, crystal, old brocades, elaborately carved walls, and magnificent chandeliers.

THE SOUTH FAÇADE FROM THE GREAT LAWN

THE BOXWOOD GARDEN

Old Westbury Gardens is best known throughout the land for its sumptuous landscaping; the seventy-acre park is filled with colorful shrubs and flowers, adorned by retaining walls, treillage, balustrades, statuary, and artificial pools. Among the many different gardens are the Boxwood Garden, with a panorama of Grecian columns and reflecting pool; the two-level walled Italian Garden; and the Ghost Walk of trained hemlock. The great south lawn with its massive gate sets off a tree-lined vista. Swans and wild ducks fill the great lake, which is surrounded by wildflower walks, and the marble temple of love. Few estates have been as blessed as the Westbury Gardens, for it was decided in 1958 to maintain the gardens as a non-profit arboretum and horticultural exhibit endowed by the J. S. Phipps Foundation. The property is presently administered by the Board of Directors of the Old Westbury Gardens, to preserve its charm and beauty for a much-admiring public.

THE MAIN ENTRANCE

A GUEST BEDROOM

DRAWING ROOM

PICKET FARM

Just off the service road of the Long Island Expressway in Jericho, a small wooden sign painted gray with white letters reads "PICKET FARM—NO TRESPASSING!" I don't know what possessed me to drive over to the Lehman house that day, September 28, 1977. I've often had a compulsion to visit a place, sensing something in the air, and never being able to explain it. I only know that a few hours later the house was gone. Three young boys were seen by the caretaker running from the blazing fire that caused the forty-room brick structure to burn to the ground in a matter of hours. I had regretted never having gotten around to photographing the inside of the house, and now it was too late. The place had been boarded up for at least ten years and though its doom seemed imminent before the fire, plans were still being made to restore it for use as a club house.

The Georgian manor had four white pillars that supported the front façade; a gracefully proportioned door and fan window stood in the center with a wrought iron balcony above. The house was originally built by A. Ludlow Kramer some time in the early 'Twenties and later bought during the 'Fourties by Allen S. Lehman, who was a partner of Lehman Brothers, and nephew of Senator Herbert H. Lehman. Designed by Julian Peabody of Peabody, Willson and Brown, the 68-acre property ran adjacent to what is now the College of Old Westbury, formerly the Ambrose Clark estate. In fall, foxhunting is still the tradition and the hounds still run through the estate's wooded acres and often use it as a check stop before going on.

I remember walking the length of the endless halls on that last day and wondering what was to become of the place; the walls had softened and were beginning to crumble. Most of the doors had been torn off their hinges and were lying on the floor covered with plaster and damp fragments of decaying carpeting. There was not one stick of furniture left in the house: vandals had made off with most of it over the years.

It was impossible to see anything on the first floor, since the windows were boarded up, but with a flashlight you could make out the order of the rooms. Terra cotta tiles were set into the floor of the main entrance hall and though most of the spindles on the banister were ripped out, the main staircase was still impressive. From what I could make out there was a ballroom or at least a very large room with French doors, now boarded up; you had to descend several steps to enter the room. A gaping hole marked the place where a mantel would have surrounded the huge fireplace. At the other end of the hall were the dining room and a study with a large oak bar like the kind you see in western movies. Some broken glass lay amid the cobwebs.

On the second floor there must have been at least twenty bedrooms including

AFTERMATH OF THE TRAGIC FIRE OF SPRING 1978

those of the servants' wing, which were much smaller in size. Several of the bedrooms were dismal, with faded floral wallpaper that was beginning to peel off in layers and fall to the floor. All of the bathrooms were completely gutted out— not one had a sink intact or a mirror unbroken. The vandals had really gone through the place, taking even the door knobs. I found the third floor the most intriguing; there was a large studio with a brick fireplace and an open glass skylight letting in lots of light. Running east and west the entire length of the house was an attic with exposed timbers. Strewn about the floor were dozens of overturned trunks and boxes filled with old clothes, curtains, and brocaded draperies with beautifully colored silk tassels. I remember pulling some of them off, knowing no one would ever come to claim them.

The bath house is still standing and before it the swimming pool, half filled, is black with decay. An abandoned greenhouse stands nearby, though all the glass is broken and only the steel frames remain. From it you can see the brick stables and garage complex in the distance. Off in the garden that once faced the house is a wooden arbor of no particular style—it is overgrown with vines and was probably once part of a rose garden. Just before entering the circular drive where the main house once stood, off to the right is a simple round brick garden house or gazebo; through its two open arched doors one can see past to the field beyond. A profusion of broken clay flower pots lie on its stone floor.

THE MAIN ENTRANCE, PICKET FARM

No simple presentation of a building's exact dimensions and lines can ever give us a total feeling of what a house once was. Only the imagination can transcend the cruel reality of the charred and twisted, ghastly and grieving ruins that are all that is left of Picket Farm.

ENTRANCE TO THE SOLARIUM

THE FRONT DOORWAY

THE CORINTHIAN FRONT ENTRANCE

FOXLAND

William Holloway

A splendid example of an ante-bellum style plantation stands majestically in a thicket of trees overlooking magnificent rolling hills in Old Westbury. Originally named Rosemary, it was designed by George A. Freeman for Foxhall P. Kene, Esq. in 1906. It was later owned by William Holloway of oil millions, and vast stock in shipping lines. He was

FOXLAND. THE FRONT DRIVE

also the great-grandson of William Russell Grace, twice mayor of New York City. Holloway renamed the house Foxland because of its abundance of foxes who roamed about the estate, so fond was he of the endangered species. Believing a hunt to be cruel sport, when one was due to run through his property he would hide the foxes in a storm tunnel until the riders were safely out of sight.

While everyone of the manor born was indulging in various whims and fancies, there were those who surrounded themselves with their favorite furred and feathered friends. Morgan had his cows, Mrs. Paul Prybal had her rats and mice, Mona Williams her peacocks strutting around the indoor swimming pool, and Frick his cages full of zoo animals. Mrs. William Holloway, I am told, drove her husband to leave for a tropical island when she filled one of the main rooms in the house with chimpanzees who leaped about, and threw bananas from tree stumps set into the floor of what had originally been a sitting room.

The main façade of the house is well composed, all in white, with simple dignified lines. Four stately pillars rise to the roof of the portico. Set way back from the main house in a thicket of trees is the now crumbling stone faced stable designed around a center courtyard. Several of the carriage barns that were part of the complex burned to the ground in recent years, probably the work of vandals. The stable area is so overgrown now that one can hardly see the entrance where the fine show horses were once housed.

FOXLAND. FROM THE AIR

Inside, the central entrance hall, though empty of all furnishings, is still impressive with its exquisite sweeping staircase, reminiscent of a "Gone With the Wind" movie set. A red and crystal Venetian glass chandelier adds the only decorative touch at the mid-level platform. Four spacious rooms open off the center hall. The furnishings have long since been dispersed to the far corners of the earth, but I shall describe the rooms as they once were: The main drawing room was originally painted white and trimmed with oaken panels. The white plaster ceiling was crowned by a festooned framed oval. An elaborate mantel had a built-in mirror, with a tracery like that of a window. Rich red damask draperies softened the windows and doors. Steinway had designed an Italian walnut piano especially for the room.

From the ceiling of the handsomely paneled dining room hung four chandeliers of a unique design of gilt baskets containing bunches of white and purple grapes. Billiard rooms were a very popular feature in many North Shore manor homes, and Foxland's was among the finest—alive with color and rich detail. Its walls were done in

99

THE DRAWING ROOM

THE STABLES

THE SWEEPING STAIRCASE, MAIN HALL

the deepest shade of purple damask; along the wall huge, wide, built-in seats were covered in matching purple leather. An immense fireplace dominated the room with a large overmantel with upper columns. Just off the billiard room through tall French doors one entered the side porch, which was once completely draped in a profusion of blooming white clematis. Today the once lovely formal flower gardens and terraced stairway are completely overgrown in a tangle of weeds and wandering vines.

The estate is now part of the New York Technical University. One can catch a fleeting glimpse of the house peeking through the trees off the Long Island Expressway just past Exit 39.

A MEADOW AT FOXLAND

AT FOXLAND, ONE OF THE LAST RIDES OF THE MEADOWBROOK HUNT CLUB

A MEDIEVAL FORTRESS FACING THE SOUND

FERGUSON CASTLE

A colorful Spanish-style castle, copied from the monasteries found throughout Europe, stood high above the harbor in Huntington. When seen from the water, the castle provided a noble panorama of Mediterranean architecture. Ferguson Castle, as it was known, was designed by Allen W. Jackson in 1908 for Mrs. Juliana Armour Ferguson. Built like a medieval fortress, it had heavy walls some three and four feet thick. One got the feeling the builder had in mind the necessity of defense against a sudden night attack. A pair of seventeenth century pillars of granite stone, with fourteenth century lions used as finials graced the fort-like entrance court at the top of the drive. After the death of Mrs. Ferguson in 1921, the house was empty for long periods and changed hands several times.

Mrs. Ferguson loved children, yet she was obsessed by the bizarre habit of collecting tombstones from childrens' graves. She gathered them up from all over Europe; all were those of children under five years old when they died, and the stones were all three hundred years old. She then had them installed in the floors, halls, entranceways, and garden of her Huntington castle.

THE GREAT HALL

RUINED COURTYARD

ANCIENT GARGOYLE

THE MAIN DINING ROOM, PAVED WITH TOMBSTONES

Mrs. Ferguson had five children of her own, who would push back the heavy ancient furnishings in the grand hall and turn it into a roller skating rink for themselves and their friends. She was so overcome with grief following the death of her son Danforth in the First World War, that as legend has it, she had a wax dummy made in his image that was placed at the head of the table each evening.

In 1916, the castle was used as a location site for the making of the original movie of Romeo and Juliet, and was rented for several weeks by Metro-Goldwyn-Mayer as a crew of several hundred people moved into the noble edifice. The valuable contents of the house included a 16th century chariot that had been built for the Emperor Maximilian, made of ornate carved ivory and set with rubies.

In 1964, Suffolk County took possession of the castle; then it stood abandoned, prey to the invasions of vandals. The castle was finally bulldozed. Rumors claiming the house to be haunted, and back taxes totaling over $100,000, not to mention the problem of heating the place, had made it a difficult property to sell.

THE TOWER COMMANDED AN IMPRESSIVE VIEW OF THE SOUND

Inside, a reception room and private elevator were passed before coming to the Great Hall, which was breathtaking in size. Two seventeenth century seated lions of Verona marble supported the entrance arcade. The Mediterranean style room was surrounded by arched porticoes where art treasures, some dating from the twelfth century, were set into the walls. The room is in the form of an atrium, and at its far end is a magnificent fountain made of brilliantly colored old Persian tiles. Inserted in one wall over the fountain was a French Gothic 15th century plaque with three niches: there is a Madonna and Child in the center and saints on either side. An old Spanish tile plaque has a colorful coat of arms, and there was a pre-Christian era Egyptian plaque that was also a museum piece.

THIS WAS THE WEST LOGGIA FACING THE POOL

At one time water splashed from a marble lion's head set into the porcelain Persian tiles of the staircase fountain. Supporting the balconies were columns of varying kinds of marble, with ancient capitals. Light filtering through the all-glass ceiling added warmth to the otherwise sombre room. At the top of the stairs were doors leading out to the open courtyard, which was once a pleasant garden. The round pool was almost completely obscured by the overgrown vines. A huge clock tower, and bell system, that used to chime on the half hour, set off the south structure of the court. In addition to the forty rooms and sixteen tiled baths, there was also a gymnasium, with a wood-beamed ceiling and steam baths—and a billiard room.

One of the outstanding rooms of the castle was the dining room, with frescoed

COLUMNED WALK WITH AUTHENTIC BYZANTINE PILLARS

ceiling and Gothic arches. It is said to have taken the artist Robert Sewell four and a half years to complete this unique ceiling with its scenes from the Bible. A tomb-like echo could be heard if you spoke while standing under the medieval chandelier with its chain made of interlocking crosses. It was here in this ominous room that the floor was paved with tombstones from children's graves; no one has ever been able to find out how or where they were acquired. Two corner pieces over the doorway are 17th century Italian marble depicting an eagle about to strike, a saint taming a lion, and a grotesque chicken. The marble capitals are of a bullock and a griffin.

Above the mantel of the huge fireplace was a sculpture of a reclining angel, alleged to be the work of Michelangelo. At the far end of the room were leaded stained glass windows reflecting the Renaissance theme of the room. The bedrooms throughout the house were austere with a cell-like atmosphere, though they all had fireplaces. The walls revealed the faded outlines of where a cross had hung in each of the twenty-two bedrooms. I am told that many of the bedspreads had a large cross embroidered in the center.

In 1964 the property was acquired by Suffolk County and opened to the public, but though thousands of people were awed by the castle's size and theatrical qualities, there were just not enough funds to restore it. In the summer of 1970, the castle met its doom in the blade of the bulldozer.

BROAD HOLLOW

Ambrose Clark Estate

Set many miles in from the main road in Old Westbury stands the Ambrose Clark estate, built in 1912. Through an arch-shaped gatehouse and on up the drive, one passes endless miles of meadows that stretch as far as the eye can see, and seem to haze into shades of purple at the horizon. There was a time when the land of Broad Hollow, as the five-hundred-acre estate is known, never felt the imprint of an automobile tire, for Ambrose Clark believed the automobile to be the invention of the devil. At the top of a hill surrounded by endless stone walls stood the white pillared forty-two-room colonial mansion. Inside, a spiral stairway rose from a red tiled foyer, beautifully lit at the top by an open glass Adam style dome. The oak paneled ballroom, which was added to the house for a visit from the Prince of Wales in 1924, is one of the main features of the building. It overlooks a terrace which is surrounded by flowering shrubs and has a view of a charming summer pavilion.

SWEEPING LAWNS AND BROAD MEADOWS WERE THE VIEW FROM THIS SIDE OF MAIN HOUSE

In its day, the house was always filled with much activity and entertaining and had the hearty flavor of the hunts. Clark thought nothing of entertaining five hundred

SKYLIGHT IN THE MAIN HALL

ALONG THE ENTRANCE LANE

at lunch: the menu was usually wild game, stuffed pigs, squab and huge roasts. Ambrose Clark, whose passion in life was horses, had his great stables built within sight of the

THE STABLES

THIS WING OF BROAD HOLLOW CONTAINED A SPECIAL BALLROOM BUILT
FOR A PARTY GIVEN THE PRINCE OF WALES IN 1924

manor house. The ivy-covered stables are constructed to form a square, in the center of which is a sawdust exercise ring. Today endless rows of stalls, drained of all life, still bear the names of such greats as Sir Echo, Mr. Biddue, Kellsboro Jack, Tea-Maker, and Birmingham, all trained by Clark. Clark's Field was once one of the finest steeplechase courses in the United States. The millionaire horseman, whose blue and yellow silks were represented on racetracks all over the world, was said to be a dashing figure as he galloped across his fields in his gray bowler, waistcoat and stock, and riding breeches. He was often seen in town with his four-in-hand, complete with a footman and bugler in attendance.

Everything centered around horses. He raised, trained and rode them from sunup to sundown until the day he died at the age of eighty-three. Clark was one of four brothers, who made their fortune in the Singer Sewing Machine Company, which they owned. Besides Broad Hollow, Clark also owned Kellsboro House, a plantation in South Carolina, a farm at Cooperstown, New York, and Melton Mowbray in England. Life as it was known on the estate came to an end in 1964 with the death of Mr. Clark. His prized horses were sold off at auction; the sumptuous furnishings were given to Lenox Hill Hospital. His outstanding collection of horse paintings went to the Saratoga museum. The estate has since been bought, and is now the State University College of Old Westbury.

In the middle of its being converted for school use, it caught fire as workmen were using a blowtorch and tar to repair the roof. All that remains of the great manor house is an empty shell, some charred brick walls, and twisted steel girders.

OVERLOOKING VIKING'S COVE

VIKINGS' COVE

The home of the late Edith Kane Baker commands one of the most breathtaking views of Long Island Sound that can be seen from the North Shore. Perched on a cliff high above the water, the sixteen-acre estate once was the gracious home of a gracious lady. Descended on her mother's side from the Brevoorts, one of the founding families of New Amsterdam, now New York, she was married to George F. Baker who, until his death in 1937, was president of New York's First National Bank. It was founded by his father, later merged to form First National City Bank, and is now Citibank, the second largest commercial bank in the world.

THERE WERE ONCE MOONLIGHT DANCES ON THE UPPER DECK OF THIS RUINED BATHHOUSE

Mrs. Baker's home on Long Island (she had two others, one in New York City and one in Tallahassee, Florida) was a fitting place for her spring and summer entertaining. In her heyday as a Long Island Grande Dame and hostess extraordinaire, an army of some twenty gardeners toiled to maintain the beautifully landscaped property. Used extensively for lawn teas, debutante balls and weddings, the grounds still reflect their former glory—charming walks with roses clinging to arched trellises, spring and summer flowers in abundance, cast iron urns, Italian statuary and manicured lawns create a mood of great beauty and serenity. However, the years since Mrs. Baker, who died at the age of 94 in 1977, entertained lavishly have taken their toll on the magnificent estate. A bath house at the bottom of a cliff overlooking the Sound has fallen into acute disrepair. A stone structure, it is now crumbling into the Sound; the upper deck of the terrace, which was one used for dancing on moonlit summer evenings, is unsafe even for standing now. The wooden balustrade which ran along the top of the building and protected party-goers from the great fall to the rocks below has all but gone, and with it the sea-wall which protected the building from erosion. The celadon green tiles which lined the dressing rooms are falling in quick succession and there hasn't been a fire in the fireplace for years.

Designed in 1914 by architects Stewart and Walker, the main house is a symphony of graceful arches. Three arches set off both the front and rear of the main wing, allowing the house to be cooled by gentle sea breezes. The sweeping marble-

THE GALLERY AT VIKING'S COVE ONCE HOUSED FINE PAINTINGS

trimmed archway leads to the front door, also arch shaped. The visitor is then greeted by a large marble staircase which, interestingly enough, is angular, providing relief from the arches, and certainly a distinct contrast. The second floor is taken up by a long sunlit gallery, with the arch theme repeated through six huge windows recessed into arches spaced equidistant from one another along its great length.

Mrs. Baker's grace and style were at once evident. A forty-foot-long blue and beige Persian rug was laid on the highly polished wood floor; four small console tables stood against the walls between the arches, which were hung with charming English prints. The main drawing room was oak paneled and the entire room, in fact, was reminiscent of an English country estate of the last century. A George II inlaid walnut circular library table stood in the center of the room, and behind the table, over the black marble fireplace, hung an 18th century hunting scene painted by Benjamin Marshall. On the same floor of Mrs. Baker's home was the dining room, with soft green and beige chinoiserie rice paper on its walls. Again the arch motif was repeated, but this time the arches were achieved by panels of wallpaper, rather than the architecture itself. Lighting the dining room is a huge bay window, which allowed guests to enjoy the passing of the yachts entering the Cove.

CHINOISERIE PANELS IN THE DINING ROOM

BRONZE
URNS

BATH HOUSE
WINDOW

ONE OF THE GUEST COTTAGES

THE WEST WING

THE REAR OF THE HOUSE COMMANDS A MAGNIFICIENT VIEW OF VIKING'S COVE

And Mrs. Baker certainly had guests. All the guest rooms were full every weekend, and dinner parties ranged from twenty select guests to eighty. Those staying at Vikings' Cove for the weekend played golf, tennis and swam at the Piping Rock Club, socially the top of the heap of the North Shore country clubs. To support this life style, Mrs. Baker was extremely fortunate in her butler, Douglas Griffin—at one time named butler of the year in *Town and Country* magazine. He oversaw a staff of eighteen when the house was running at its height—chamber maids, upstairs maids, downstairs maids, footmen, scullery maids and so on. He was the only one allowed to polish the silver—Mrs. Baker's silver collection was superb, to say the least. And it was housed in a walk-in safe off the butler's pantry. The Duke and Duchess of Windsor were annual guests of Mrs. Baker's, bringing with them their own cook, valet, maid and chauffeur. Not that they didn't have the utmost faith in the service Mr. Griffin and his staff provided, but because they never went anywhere without them.

Most bankers are Republicans, and the Bakers are no exception. The last really big dinner party Mrs. Baker was able to give was for Barry Goldwater in 1964, the year of his abortive run for the presidency of the United States. Mr. Griffin was on holiday in Britain, and was called back by Mrs. Baker for this gala affair. An indication of Mrs. Baker's life style and indeed, her housekeeping meticulousness can be found in the master bedroom suite of Vikings' Cove. The whole room was done in white satin; all the furniture and even the bed were upholstered with it. The walls are in three dimensional plaster work, depicting tropical flowers.

FROM THIS DOORWAY ONE APPROACHED THE FORMAL ROSE GARDENS

With all her grace and style, not to mention social prominence, Mrs. Baker was not without her personal tragedies. And even after her death, the family has had another. In 1949, Grenville "Beans" Baker was found shot to death on a lonely road on the estate in Florida. Rumor has it that he was shot by a man who was jealous of his association with a lovely young woman, with whom the assassin was also involved. The Grenville Baker Ball, in his honor, is still *the* social event on the North Shore of Long Island, but, interestingly enough, it has never taken place at Vikings' Cove. One must wonder whether this might be because the family prefers to forget his unfortunate and untimely death.

Mr. and Mrs. William Woodward attended their last dinner party together at the Bakers' home, and that night Mr. Woodward met his death by shotgun. Last year, after Mrs. Baker's death, her son, George F. Baker II was found dead of a gunshot wound, an apparent suicide. F. Scott Fitzgerald was right—the rich ARE different from the rest of us.

REGENCY FRESCOS IN THE OVAL ROOM (SHOWN ON PAGE 123)

THE W. C. BIRD ESTATE

I first visited the W. C. Bird mansion as a child, before the invasion of housing projects. In those days I spent my weekends with friends whose parents worked on the huge estates. One could walk for miles through endless gardens, and grand alleys of linden and cherry trees that were often ended by imposing gates and surrounded by miles of

ivy covered walls. I was enchanted by the heavy mist that would blanket the vast meadows in the still-warm autumn mornings. On foggy days there was always the haunting rhythmic sound of the foghorns, that came from beyond the cliffs. It was on such a morning that I came upon what appeared to be an abandoned palace.

Vines and overgrown weeds had almost completely obscured the arch-shaped porticoed entrance. The heavy twelve-foot door was open. Alone inside, I was met by a chill of cold stagnant air, and the smells that accumulate in empty houses. Before me were the remains of another world, and I tried to imagine for a moment the breathtaking beauty that must have existed here. The house, though empty for over twenty years, had a subtle, yet disturbing beauty. The structures, now reduced to

THE ATRIUM COURTYARD (SHOWN ON PAGE 121) IN 1916

powdered stone, gave the center court the appearance of melting, diffusing the sculptured patterns of cupids and garlands of flowers that clung to the walls in an effort to remain beautiful. Beams of light came through the all-glass roof of an atrium courtyard. Most of the glass had been smashed, letting in the corroding wind and rain. In the center of the room stood the shattered remains of a marble fountain. The entire floor was covered with pieces of broken plaster and fragments of wood that had fallen or been thrown by vandals.

A huge pipe organ was enclosed in the walls surrounding the room; parts of the intricate plaster grilles that concealed it had been stripped away, baring towering pipes that reached up to the third floor. A forbidding stillness hung over everything, as though to respect the final tragedy that was yet to come. To the left was a great hall where several marble steps led to the lower level. On one side was the grand ballroom, with faded red tapestries hanging by a thread from rusty brass fixtures. Huge French doors opened out onto a terrace that overlooked a now-empty pool. The ballroom was decorated with carved wood dolphins, griffins and cupids that danced along the tops of the walls and ceiling. A ten foot door opened to a handsomely paneled study, where remnants of a delicately arched ceiling still lingered. Two moldering grand pianos stood at the far end of what must have once been a music room.

The main drawing room was breathtakingly beautiful for what it must have been; the oval shaped room was completely covered with colorful hand-painted murals of the Regency style, copied from the royal palaces found in Europe. Most of the paint had begun to crumble to the floor, yet there was a magic retained in the walls. Great

OLD VIEW OF OVAL ROOM

Palladian windows overlooked balustraded formal gardens, and overgrown vines began to work their way into the house through the broken glass. The main dining room could have seated at least a hundred guests at a time.

The story of the Wallace C. Bird mansion is probably the most tragic and macabre of the stories of ruined houses on the North Shore. It was originally built in 1915 by C. K. G. Billings, a utilities magnate, art collector and sportsman. W. C. Bird bought Farnsworth, as it was called in 1924, for his wife, Winifred Bird. The house, designed by Guy Lowell, was said to be one of the finest examples of Georgian architecture, though the interiors were reminiscent of an Italian villa. For many years it was hailed as one of the showplaces of the country, and was the scene of many gala affairs. At one, a troupe of circus horses is said to have been hired to perform on the front lawn for the guests.

Things came to an end on June 4, 1940 when Mr. Bird lost his life when his private plane went out of control. It crashed not far from his home. Mrs. Bird then had the remains of her husband's plane crated and placed down in the basement. From that day on the house was boarded up and never lived in again. Years passed, and time took its toll. The vandals came, and senseless destruction followed; all the priceless furnishings were stolen one by one, or smashed to bits. For almost a quarter of a century Mrs. Bird, a known drug addict, traveled about Europe, leaving the house unattended. She was murdered by her doctor companion in 1961 and since there were no heirs, the mansion was condemned as a liability to the property. And so the fabled palace built to last five hundred years succumbed to the impact of the bulldozer.

123

LAWN OVERLOOKING CENTER ISLAND

OAKLEY COURT

There is a feeling of mild expectation as one drives along the manicured drive to Oakley Court. There is nothing along the way to indicate what you might find at the end, for so often all that remains of a mansion is a leveled foundation or a charred and twisted pile of timbers. Oakley Court, however, is truly a home of quiet stately elegance with its unmatched sweeping view overlooking Oyster Bay Harbor and Centre Island. Designed by Henry Corse in 1936, it is built on the second highest point in Long Island. It was probably one of the last of the great manor houses to go up during the Gold Coast period. Built originally by Mrs. Whatson Dickerman, it was later owned by Alfred Vanderbilt, and Cornelius Vanderbilt Whitney.

The forty-two-acre estate grounds are extensively landscaped with beautiful trees

THE FRONT COURT

and shrubbery; towering rhododendron bushes line the end of the drive and there are also azalea, laurel, evergreens and climbing ivy to soften the lines of the house. At the bottom of a terraced garden are a sixty-five-foot marble swimming pool and two small reflecting lily ponds. In spring one is greeted by the fragrant lavender lushness of wisteria that all but covers the heavy oak front door. The whitewashed brick English Tudor manor house is set off with muted colorful Ludowice tile. There are steel casements and leaded glass windows throughout.

The music room, as it was known, is one of the most impressive rooms built anywhere, with its twenty-foot cathedral beamed ceiling and seven-foot-high fireplace. The room is enhanced by two crystal chandeliers, wide-board pegged oak floors, and two large alcoves which once contained a pipe organ. Adjoining the music room is the loggia, one of the most inviting and charming rooms in the house. Its walls, originally oak beams, are painted a soft mellow blue, with leaded glass windows, and Gothic doors that open out to the garden. Hanging plants and potted palms complement the wicker furnishings. Upstairs there are six bedroom suites and a child's nursery, all reminiscent of an English country farm house. There are little alcoves and marble fireplaces set into niches. Some of the ceilings are at odd angles to give variety to the rooms. Richly carved 18th century four poster beds and fine English antiques and hooked rugs are in keeping with the style of the house.

Oakley Court was recently the scene of much of the filming of the movie version of "Hair." As many as 300 people including extras and crew, filled the 40 or so rooms. A re-creation of a lavish 'Sixties debutante ball was staged on a lawn to the west of the house. A huge yellow and white tassel-trimmed tent was set up to shelter guests, and classic urns filled with matching colored flowers were placed everywhere. At one end of the garden a Victorian wrought iron gazebo made a romantic background for the

THE SOUTH WING FROM THE REFLECTING POOL

dancing ballerinas who performed a scene. A stage was set up for the orchestra and a
palm-trimmed dance floor completed the set. Since the party was to take place in June
and it was in reality December when filmed, thousands of plastic leaves had to be stapled

THE SOLARIUM

THE DINING ROOM

to the bare trees to create the illusion of spring. The camera did not pick up the blue and purple extras who were freezing in their strapless gowns. By the time snow started to fall Hollywood ran out of tricks!

THE MAIN DRAWING ROOM

MEUDON

Meudon by any standard was a palace; it was a replica of the famous Meudon palace located just outside of Paris, France. Designed by Charles P. H. Gilbert at the turn of the century, its 300 terraced acres were landscaped to provide an engaging view of the Sound. William D. Guthrie built the 80-room Meudon as a country home for himself and his family. The noted lawyer to the Rockefeller clan had accumulated millions by managing the intricate affairs of great corporations. He was also a well-known writer on the subject of political and legal topics. Guthrie, together with John E. Aldred, who went on to build Ormston House nearby, bought and demolished 60 homes and stores that comprised the village of Lattingtown, which had been in the way of their building plans.

PILLARS SURROUNDING THE REFLECTING POOL

MARBLE LIONS GUARD THE MAIN ENTRANCE

Shield-bearing marble lions stood guard outside the entrance of the neo-classic manor, while six Corinthian columns supported the main façade.

A limestone balustrade ran along the entire top of the house and outlined the terrace that surrounded its base. The grounds provided a spectacular setting for the endless rounds of parties that were given at Meudon in its heyday. There were secluded arbors with marble seats and a handsome pergola, its lines lost amidst its lush mantle of tea roses in spring. At one time over 40 gardeners were kept busy tending Meudon's vast expanse of trees, shrubs, gardens and banks of wall flowers. A seemingly endless stone staircase stretched from the terrace of the main house and terminated with a marble water lily pool surrounded by vari-colored blooms. There were flower gardens with gravel walks bordered by herbaceous plants, hollyhocks, delphiniums, phlox, jasmines and dahlias.

An iron-railed bridge nearby made it possible for cars and horses to cross the churning creek to where the spacious grey and white wood frame bath house still stands on the edge of the beach. At one time the *Meudon III*, a 38-foot power cruiser, unique in its day, was moored at the private dock. The brick and stucco dairy barn is built around four sides of a court; there were 23 cow tieups, 4 box stalls, 2 bull pens, a hay loft, 12 stalls for the riding horses, and spacious cottages for the help. Nearby a group of farm buildings included a poultry house, corn crib, brooder houses, farm garages, storage shed and turkey house.

BATH HOUSE ON THE SHORE

William Guthrie died in 1944 at the age of ninety-two; at about that time the estate began its decline, with the war calling away most of the help and taxes ever on the increase. His widow, Ella Fuller Guthrie, lived to be 100 years old and died in the house while, I am told, the manor had fallen to ruin all about her. Following her death in 1958, many of the furnishings, tapestries and art objects were placed on the auction block. I had all but given up ever finding any existing photographs of Meudon as it once looked in its day, for most often, families disenchanted with the burden of taxes and vandalism, are forced to destroy the houses, and old picture albums are lost or misplaced in the process of moving from place to place. As luck would have it, Mrs. Marion Johnson, the granddaughter of William Guthrie, still lives on the estate in one of the original buildings that overlooks a small pond.

She called one day to say she'd found the old leather bound album that had been missing for so long. When I saw it for the first time, it was like looking into another world. The album had faded with age and was crumbling as we looked through it together. On the cover, written in large gold letters, was the name Meudon. Inside, it contained large mounted prints of all of the main rooms and gardens. As Mrs. Johnson went through each page, she talked nostalgically about what it was like to grow up in such a splendid house as a child. "We used to dive all over the furniture, and tumble about those awesome bear and lion fur rugs, with those sharp fangs glaring out at us. . . . Those were wonderful times," she said, "Somehow you think it will go on forever, but it's all gone now."

She described the quiet order of things in the vast greenhouses, the intoxicating smell of the espaliered fruit trees, camellias and flourishing palms and chrysanthemums. "I used to love the long wooden arbor with all those lush blue and white

THE BARONIAL RECEPTION HALL

grapes cascading down. I've never tasted anything so wonderful since."

From the photographs in the album we can explore the house. Inside, as you entered through a heavy bronze and glass door, there was a baronial reception hall set off by a wide carved oak staircase. Above it hung an 18th century tapestry of "Diana Resting after the Chase." All about the room were sumptuous furnishings, including many ornately carved Elizabethan pieces. A pair of tiger skin rugs with mounted heads facing each other lay on carpeted floor. Dominating one wall was a handsome Carrara marble Italian Renaissance wall fountain. Victorian lamps with silk pleated and fringed shades added warmth to the otherwise sombre room. The library, where Guthrie spent much of his time writing, also housed his valuable collection of law books. It was a comfortable room with heavy overstuffed chairs and a leather tufted iron railing around the fireplace for one to put one's feet up on cold winter days. On either side of the fireplace stood an 18th century set of globes, one celestial, the other terrestrial. A pair of foo dogs on top of the bookcases stood in front of a stained glass window.

A rounded glass-roofed solarium extended out just to the left of the front entrance. It was a cheerful room with great tubs of Boston ferns, palms and dark green Victorian wicker furniture, and a small marble fountain set into the floor. Fanciful lattice-work walls gave it an outdoor garden feeling. Upstairs, the master bedroom was spacious and had a beautiful view of the Sound and terraced gardens, but the furnishings were undistinguished, aside from the draped canopy that hung over the twin beds. A glass-topped dressing table was covered with a profusion of silver and gold crystal boudoir jars, and an antique brush set. Overhead, a ceiling fixture with rose

THE LIBRARY

A GUEST BEDROOM

colored silk pleated shades hung down from a brace rod. Many of the guest bedrooms were French in feeling with ornamental plaster work walls; 22 house servants kept the rooms filled with fresh flowers brought in daily from the cutting gardens. All about the

THE MASTER BEDROOM

THE PALM CONSERVATORY

room were delicate Alençon and Belgian lace ruffled pillows that lay on comfortable pastel chairs. Meudon was bulldozed in the early 'Sixties; by the time I had found it, all that remained of its former grandeur was a row of limestone pillars barely held together by a wooden semi-circular frame. It was an open lonely place, revealing its secrets only in riddles. The terraced gardens were a mass of weeds bearing no resemblance to their former beauty. High above, a stone balustrade marked the place where the magnificent manor house once stood. Bleak leafless trees rose up from the tangled swamp grass.

A large moon-shaped pool reflected the stone colonnade and occasional meanderings of clouds in its murky water. Several pedestals made of tiny stones stood in the bottom of the pool. They were probably once used to support statues that are now long gone. Stretching out from another large pool nearby is a series of aqueducts or channels that runs from one end of the estate to where the main gate still stands. A large rusty wheel, covered with seaweed, extends out from one corner of the pool. It was used to control the water flowing in from the salt water creek nearby. Today the pillars retain some memory of what was, quiet reminders of another time too few people remember.

135

J. P. MORGAN ESTATE

The former residence of John Pierpont Morgan stands at the far north end of East Island. One must cross a guarded stone bridge to get to the red brick Georgian mansion, a stately dwelling with 52 rooms that was Morgan's home until his death in 1943. As recorded in *A History of Glen Cove* by Bob Coles and the late Peter Van Santvoord, published in 1968, Glen Cove received its share of prominent and wealthy men. The earliest of them settled near Steamboat Landing, where the names Appleby, Lafarge, Barlow, and Ladew can be found on the early maps.

THE WEST LOGGIA, FACING THE SOUND

J. P. Morgan, son of the great financier of the same name, purchased East Island and Dasoris Pond from Mr. and Mrs. Thomas W. Joyce in 1909 for some $10,000. He then developed a palatial estate known as Matinecock Point on the Island, that consisted of 110 acres and included a large pond of equal size. One had to cross a medieval-style stone bridge complete with 24-hour guard, who stood watch in Morgan's little guard house overlooking the churning water. Peace and quiet could be found here for the emperor of a banking house, whose word could cause doom to mighty industries.

Unusual for a stately mansion, a herd of cows were always grazing in the gardens and on the lawns surrounding Morgan's home. Morgan claimed he found the sight of them restful. He enjoyed the peace of his estate until it was shattered one night in 1915, when a young German instructor, Frank Holt, who must have been deranged, forced his way into the house and fired two shots into Morgan's body at close range with a revolver. It was Morgan's butler who is credited with having jumped the would-be assassin, thereby saving his employer's life. While awaiting trial for attempted murder, Holt committed suicide in his Mineola jail. Morgan, who survived, was back on the job at Morgan and Company two months after the incident, and his financial wizardry kept his firm intact during the shaky times of World War One.

Known for his philanthropic activities, Morgan is best known for the renowned art collection and wing that houses it at the Metropolitan Museum of Art. For Glen Cove residents he also provided the Morgan Memorial Park, which is still maintained by the board of trustees of the Morgan family. The interiors of the mansion that was his home were luxuriously furnished with many gleaming crystal chandeliers and beautifully draped French doors. The splendor of a French chateau is reflected in the dining room, painted a pale dark green, with 14K gold accents. At Christmas, Morgan held lavish parties, gathering all his children and grandchildren around a glittering tree heaped with presents, as he read from Dickens.

Outside on the grounds, manicured lawns and swaying trees met the water's edge, where his 343-foot yacht, the fabulous *Corsair*, once docked. It had a crew of 60 men and slept 84 passengers. The dock itself was 400 feet long, to accommodate the *Corsair*. Morgan's head steward, Charles Irvine, was often called upon to cook for 250 people while on board and claimed that corned beef and cabbage was one of Mr. Morgan's favorite meals. Morgan commuted to his Wall Street offices each day on a small steam powered boat called the *Nevette*, that carried a crew of ten men.

Morgan died before seeing his home taken over by the Soviet government. They filled the mansion with cheap and gaudy furniture and threw bottles and litter on his once-prized lawns. The multi-million-dollar estate was sold for back taxes totaling a mere $30,000 back in 1951 and has since been taken over by a Catholic order. It is now a convent surrounded by a modern housing development.

SALUTATIONS

Junius Spencer Morgan

Connected to the mainland near Lattingtown by a short causeway is West Island, or Dasoris Island as some call it. An aerial view best shows the splendid gardens and baronial layout of Salutations, former estate of the late Junius Spencer Morgan, who died in 1960. The grandson of financier J. Pierpont Morgan built the house in 1929 on the Morgans' adjoining island, which consists of 20 acres overlooking the Sound. Until recently the estate was one of the last vestiges of unchanged Gold Coast splendor. Following the death of Mrs. Louise C. Morgan, the entire estate was put up for sale and its contents auctioned off in a spectacular four day sale in 1974 that brought in unexpected millions.

Junius Morgan, heir to his grandfather's banking fortune, was a noted yachtsman, and his love for the sea was reflected in his vast collection of ship models enclosed in glass display cases. The models also were sold at auction. The main house, built of heavy stone, was on the Gothic order; massive oak doors at the front led to a center courtyard drive. Inside, dark paneling gave the interiors a much too somber mood. An interesting feature in the house is the main hall entrance, where seven large glassed-in Ming pottery figures of Chinese officials were set in wall niches. The main drawing room contained a rare twelve-paneled Coromandel screen along with many fine pieces of English furnishings, including a silver collection. The Morgan children had their own doll house to play with: a miniature copy of Salutations seven feet high and complete with porcelain furnishings and electrically-lit tiny chandeliers.

Mrs. Morgan was known for her prized show dogs. She had extensive kennels built alongside the main house. The animals would begin to bark the moment anyone set foot on the private island. Today the estate is still privately owned, and though the gardens have been simplified, it is maintained as in the old days.

A MOROCCAN GAZEBO STANDS ON THE NORTHWEST POINT OF THE ISLAND

TENNIS COURT AND SWIMMING POOL COMPLEX. THE MAIN HOUSE IS TO THE LEFT

GREENTREE

John Hay Whitney Estate

The closest I ever got to Greentree, one of the two vast Whitney compounds, was one thousand feet as I flew over it in a small private plane. It seems that no one is ever permitted to photograph the property except family members and their friends. Still, what I could see was impressive. Greentree is owned by famous sportsman, socialite, and entrepreneur John Hay "Jock" Whitney, the grandson of William C. Whitney. It is a world unto itself and stands apart from most other Gold Coast estates in that it is intact and maintained as in the old days. In the quiet of the original 500 secluded acres and manicured lawns there is the 32-room sprawling grey and white shingled colonial house. It is a many-chambered home with twelve master bedrooms and ten baths, eighteen fireplaces, and rambling wings to house the French butler, valets, footman, cooks, chamber maids, gardeners, handymen and chauffeur. There is also a partly enclosed porch, and two terraces facing the gardens.

The estate's greatest glory is the famous racing stables and breeding farm that Whitney owned along with his sister, the late Mrs. Joan Payson, of party-giving fame. Whitney's great love of horses won him the national polo title in 1935 and 1936. He also bred the 1953 horse of the year, which won $570,165 that season. One could write columns on Jock Whitney: his accomplishments seem almost endless. This is true of the entire Whitney family and all its descendants. It was William Collins Whitney who was the founding father of the Whitney clan and it was he who established the family fortune, second only to that of the Rockefellers. W. C. Whitney had managed to attain a monopoly on the transportation system in New York City and managed to do what no one else has done since; that is, to make a fortune at it. Replacing horse drawn vehicles with the electric trolley cars around the turn of the century was the result of his efforts. He also had a hand in politics, managing the presidential campaign and was instrumental in Grover Cleveland's return to the White House. Whitney then went on to persuade the U.S. Navy to replace wooden sailboats with a modern steam-powered fleet made of steel. Following that, he invested in a railroad line, crossing paths, as it were, with the powerful Jay Gould and Commodore Vanderbilt. He then conceived the idea of a transcontinental railway to promote trade with China. William C. Whitney had two sons, Harry Payne Whitney and William Payne Whitney, who built Greentree.

There are two distinct branches of the Whitney dynasty. This came about due to the fact that William C. Whitney remained a widower for three years after his wife died, then shocked the family when he decided to remarry. This caused a major split in the family allegiance, for his former brother-in-law Oliver Payne was outraged. The two brothers went their separate ways. William Payne, in protest over his father's remarriage, dropped his first name, becoming Payne Whitney minus the "William." This confused the horse-raising world and everyone else, because the last names were still similar. And so we have the Whitneys of Greentree in Manhasset and the Whitneys of Old Westbury. Upon William C. Whitney's death in 1904, his two sons inherited some $300,000,000, three hundred million dollars. Though some believe that their father was shot one night at the opera, the family claims that he died of a burst appendix. As fate would have it—Payne Whitney died of a heart attack while playing tennis at his Greentree court in Manhasset. In keeping with his passion for the game, he was buried in his white tennis flannels. Harry Payne Whitney of Westbury House died when he ran from a game at his indoor court down to the stables a mile away to be with his prized mare as she gave birth to a foal. He was then stricken with pneumonia and died several days later.

John Hay "Jock" Whitney became heir to one of the nation's greatest fortunes when his father Payne Whitney died in 1927. He also inherited the ability to succeed at just about everything he put his mind to. Among his contributions were J. H. Whitney & Co., an investment firm. He was also publisher of the *New York Herald Tribune* and Ambassador to the Court of St. James. One must make note here of his Hollywood ventures: he, along with David O. Selznik produced the most successful film in history, "Gone With The Wind." It was he who bought up the movie rights from Margaret

Mitchell for $50,000. Despite these demanding enterprises, Whitney found time to play the role of big game hunter and sportsman socialite, diplomat, philanthropist, and playboy. Today he lives in a world of private luxury, dividing his time between his office in New York and six estates he owns in Augusta, Georgia, Lexington, Kentucky, Thomasville, Georgia, Saratoga Springs, New York, Fisher's Island and Manhasset, Long Island.

The entrance to Greentree is simple, almost humble; a whitewashed wooden fence surrounds the 500-acre estate. As the bluestone drive curves around to the left, one passes an orchard on the right and a massive glass palm conservatory filled with luxuriant tropical palms and exotic flowering plants. Well-clipped hedges and laurel bushes surround the indoor tennis complex. It is a huge colonial-style building, as in the main house. The corners are softened by climbing ivy. The size of the place is overpowering; the tallest man would be dwarfed by its proportions. Inside the all-glass-roofed court, heads of deer, boar and other wildlife reflect the big game hunting days of the owner. There is a balcony lounge with dressing rooms for guests at either end, overlooking a perfectly maintained clay tennis court. Below, on another level, is the Olympic-size indoor swimming pool.

Many outbuildings and guest cottages are well placed amid the expansive lawns. A shingled cow barn containing 12 stanchions and 6 calving pens creates a picturesque scene next to the tiled silo, hay loft, dairy barn, corn cribs and wooden chicken house. The gardens are still maintained by some 22 gardeners, something unheard of in this day. On the south side is a wisteria-covered portico that separates an old English garden with a beautiful lily pond and broad fountain in its center. Magnolia and lilac bushes set off the marble seats and other garden statuary.

HARRY PAYNE WHITNEY ESTATE

In Old Westbury, it was Harry Payne Whitney and his son Cornelius Vanderbilt Whitney who presided over one thousand acres of rolling hills and five miles of bridle paths. Harry Payne Whitney married Gertrude Vanderbilt, the famous sculptress who established the Whitney Museum of American Art when her collection was rejected by the Metropolitan Museum of Art along with the funds that were to be used to add a new wing to house it. Her neo-classic one-story studio, designed by Delano and Aldrich, was considered an architectural triumph. Tucked away amid massive laurel trees, it is surrounded by a beautiful gardens and many stone, bronze and clay statues done by Mrs. Whitney and some by the many students she patronized and allowed to work in her

SOUTH WING. AN HISTORIC OLD HOUSE MOVED FROM ROSLYN

secluded studio. Stretching north the entire length of the garden is a long narrow reflecting pond and swimming pool made of thousands of tiny stones set by hand. In spring, wisteria cascades down from the teakwood pergola that faces the classic building.

To peek in through the French glass doors is like looking into the past, for everything is exactly as it was fifty years ago. Hanging above a massive fireplace is a huge painting of Mrs. Whitney as a beautiful young woman. About the room are comfortable overstuffed couches and chairs, and statues and other works of art crowd the room. There is a legend that back in the 'Forties an admirer of Mrs. Whitney sculpted a nude statue of her, and that on the day he was to unveil his tribute to his love for her, she failed to show up. Overcome with grief, it is said, he climbed the twelve story water tower nearby on the estate and jumped to his death. The statue is still there, lying forgotten in the garden, boarded up and covered with ivy. There is more mystery to the water tower. Neighbors claim that it is haunted by the ghost of the dead artist. Now boarded up too, its base surrounded by a barbed wire fence, the gaunt lonely outpost can be seen for miles around. I once climbed to the top of it on a dare back in the 'Fifties. It was a dangerous place even then. Most of the wooden steps were rotted out and all the windows had been broken by vandals so the walls were damp with decay. There was the smell of unseen dead things lying in the stagnant water below. You could look down the center shaft to a seemingly bottomless pit where some kind of pump or generator was

GERTRUDE VANDERBILT WHITNEY'S PRIVATE ART STUDIO

rusting away in the darkness. At the very top was an open porch with arched windows and an iron platform railing all around.

You could reach it by climbing a tiny ladder up through the roof. The view was breathtaking—you could see the Empire State Building to the west, Connecticut to the north and the Atlantic Ocean to the south. The wind was so powerful that you had to hold on to keep from falling hundreds of feet below. One curious thing about the place was that on several of the levels on the way up there were iron rings set into the stucco walls, with chains hanging from them. On the floor below, amidst the debris left by rodents and stray animals accumulated over the years, there were piles of bones—perhaps those of dogs or other large animals. No one seems to have any idea how they got there, though I'm told that the government used the tower as a lookout post during the Second World War to search for enemy planes.

From Post Road, one of the main roads that runs through Old Westbury, one can still drive past the rambling Tudor-style racing stable that was famous in its day for the seventy-two prize horses that were housed there, along with a fine collection of turn-of-the-century carriages and polo carts that are long gone. The main house, built on the third highest point on Long Island, is a Georgian brick manor with six white pillars overlooking a golf course that today takes up much of the remaining land. The estate was the scene of the highly publicized custody battle over Gloria Vanderbilt. The property is owned by the Old Westbury Golf and Country Club. There have been many major changes since they took it over in 1958. An Olympic-sized free-form swimming

145

THE TENNIS COURT

pool was added just off the terraced west wing, where two of the original reflecting pools remain. As a club, all of the original buildings are put to good use, including the outstanding indoor tennis complex that is enjoyed by members all hours of the day. The fabulous stables, though unchanged from the outside, house many classrooms used by students of New York Tech.

RACING STABLES

LOVER'S LEAP

THE HAUNTED WATER TOWER

CAUMSETT

The Marshall Field Estate

Caumsett, one of the grandest and largest of the Gold Coast estates, was a spacious, well-ordered world unto itself. One would scarcely believe this to be Long Island, as its majestic cliffs rivaling those of the Big Sur on the West Coast rise up hundreds of feet from Long Island Sound. Though today the estate is a ghost of its former self, its cliffs and spacious woodlands and open meadows remain unchanged.

It was built by Marshall Field III, third-generation heir to the multi-million-dollar Chicago mercantile fortune that bore his grandfather's name. Field was a hospitable and gracious host. Grand and colorful parties were staged on the extensive lawns and vistas for his often famous and noted guests—including Fred Astaire, who danced to the music of Meyer Davis at one affair. The luxury yachts of Field's friends docked at the end of a long pier lit by strings of colorful Japanese lanterns. Close by, a beach house was a popular spot with its oval emerald green pool.

Field, who had spent a good deal of his life in England, bought the 1,750 acres of Caumsett in 1922, and named it after a Matinecock Indian word meaning "place by a hard rock." This tribe once occupied the site. Though born of great wealth and power, Field was driven by a need to contribute something worthwhile to his fellow men. He founded two newspapers. One evening paper in New York failed when he tried to operate it without advertising, but the other, the *Chicago Sun*, did well and later merged to become the still more successful *Sun Times.*

Like a feudal lord, Field maintained a sense of responsibility toward the people who worked for him. At Christmas time a party was held in the main house for all the children who lived on the estate, with Field himself playing Santa. He made a point of finding out what each child had hoped to find under the yuletide tree. He then mingled with his employees and at the end of the evening there would be a banquet for them in the formal dining room. Once during a shattering storm he invited some of the families whose cottages were in danger of flooding to stay the night in the main house.

THE MAIN STAIR HALL

THE RACING STABLES

THE DAIRY BARN

THE MAIN HOUSE FACING THE SOUND

Field, who was influenced by British gentry, had his footmen, valet and well-trained English and Scottish domestic help. A French chef ran the vast kitchens that dominated the entire east wing of the house. One of the remaining staff members, who is now in his 80's, recalls that visiting valets would polish the soles of guests' boots and that the daily newspaper would only be presented to his employer after it had been folded, pressed and ironed, an old English tradition.

The fifty-room main house, originally designed by John Russell Pope, is classic brick Georgian with limestone trim, though its balanced proportions were ruined when one entire wing containing the ballroom was removed in the 'Fifties. One of the most impressive buildings on the estate is the Georgian brick stable. Field, a prominent polo player in his day, had it designed around a center court: one has to pass a wrought iron gate to enter. Today its clock towers, Adam-style windows and fanlights over the main doors begin to show signs of neglect. Inside, spacious stalls run the length of a long tiled hall; all of the hardware and finials are solid brass.

Caumsett was at one time completely self-supporting. It had its own water and electrical supply. There was a hospital barn and live-in veterinarian for ailing cows, a plant to process the milk, cream and cheese. All of the help each received a quart of milk each day. Vegetable gardens supplied most of the food; there were vast cutting gardens

THE BALLROOM

and greenhouses to keep the rooms in the main house filled with fresh bouquets at all times. Pheasants still roam the miles of woodlands where at one time pheasant and skeet shooting were a popular sport of visiting guests.

Today many of the outbuildings and guest cottages, some almost mansions in their own right, are the haunt of squirrels, rodents and stray birds. Still, the overall impression of the place is breathtaking as one drives past the progression of stately pines, locust and oak trees that flourish here. The elements have completely worn away the white paint on the picturesque colonial barns and stables, revealing sturdy Georgian cypress shingles. At one time they housed 80 head of prized cattle, one of them a blue-blooded Guernsey that held the breed's milk-yielding record. It once took 85 men to run the grounds alone; George Walker, the estate's foreman, still works on the estate, though today most of his time is spent trying to keep out trespassers. Heavy chains securing the gates have done little to keep out vandals, who have mutilated the statuary and shattered the glass of the once magnificent greenhouses.

At one time Field raised his prized chrysanthemums there. There are also fragrant rose gardens surrounding the lawns of the main house. Today those gardens are lost beneath a tangle of weeds and the sunken gardens to the west have long since been reclaimed by the wilderness. The ornate wrought iron gates have rusted beyond repair.

Things have changed since Marshall Field's death in 1959. The property was bought in 1961 by the Long Island State Park Commission, and after being closed to the public since that time, its days of hibernation seem to be over. Once again people are welcome to roam about the grounds as they once were when Field was the reigning lord.

Today the main house is closed, its manorial windows are boarded up with plywood, and its future is uncertain, though the estate is still one of Long Island's most beautiful preserves and provides a vivid record of Gold Coast history.

DETAIL OF ONE OF THE MAIN WROUGHT IRON GATES

DUCKS AT THE MOAT SURROUNDING THE ENTRANCE COURT

EASTFAIR

"Eastfair" one of the North Shore Medieval style castles, complete with moat and resident dragon, was built by Sherman Fairchild in 1931, designed by R. A. Gallamore and Frank J. Forster

THE MAIN HALL

SEA WALL FACING THE SOUND

FALAISE

LIVING ROOM
Nassau County Department of Recreation and Parks

It is believed that, though Fitzgerald chose the names East Egg and West Egg for his popular novel, he was in fact describing Kings Point and Sands Point. Some of the largest estates built during the period can still be found there to this day. Falaise is a world unto itself; the estate has remained relatively untouched, as it is impossible to get behind the two huge gates that guard the entrance. Two of the Gothic-style manor houses rise up from the cliffs and can be seen from the water. They provide a striking reminder of days past to yachtsmen as they sail by. The smaller of the manor houses was designed by architect Frederich Sterner in 1923 for the late Captain Harry F. Guggenheim, who was instrumental in the promotion of aviation during its development in the 'Twenties and 'Thirties. Charles Lindbergh, who became a close friend of Guggenheim after his historic flight across the Atlantic, spent much of his time at the Château and wrote his epic book *We* while staying there. Guggenheim's interests followed a wide range; he served as Ambassador to Cuba, and was president of the Solomon R. Guggenheim Museum. He and his third wife Alicia Patterson together developed *Newsday*, now considered one of America's great daily newspapers.

A long winding drive that goes on for several miles leads to a sheltered cobblestone courtyard entrance with a wrought iron gate at the front. Set high above a cliff, the Norman-style brick manor has turrets, steep slate roofs, dormers, and casement windows.

DINING ROOM

It is one of the last remaining unaltered manor houses left from the period of transplanting European fragments into the great homes, and of filling these homes with

MASTER BEDROOM

DOORWAY, MAIN ENTRANCE

THE MAIN ENTRANCE

bowls of fresh flowers that were brought in from the greenhouses year round to perfume the house.

To this day the dining room is set as though guests are to arrive at any moment

THE CARRIAGE HOUSE COURT YARD

for a formal dinner. The table is set with gold-encrusted Minton china bearing the crest of Mr. Guggenheim, as he was Ambassador to Cuba during President Herbert Hoover's Administration.

The medieval atmosphere is enhanced by an arcaded loggia that faces the Sound side of the building. The twenty-six rooms are furnished with fine and rare 16th and 17th century French and Spanish pieces acquired by the Captain on his many trips abroad. Many great art treasures decorate the interiors: paintings and religious sculptures, among them a Florentine sculpture of St. John the Baptist by Andrea Della Robbia and a statue, "The Black Venus," by Paul Gauguin. There are also colorful tiles, ironwork and a vast collection of silver racing trophies found throughout the house. The living room is dominated by a gigantic carved stone fireplace under a Flemish tapestry depicting a medieval town, and fanciful pelicans and hawks. Also found in the room is a bronze plaque hidden behind the corner of the mantelpiece, which reads "Goddard: America's father of the space age." Like so many of the North Shore elite, Guggenheim's passion was thoroughbred breeding and racing; by climbing down a winding stairway one could enter his trophy room where his prized collection of gleaming silver urns and platters recalling his triumphs on the racetrack are displayed. Off one of the rooms in a sheltered walled court is a magnificent emerald green pool with garden statues around its edge.

"Falaise" (The French word for cliff and the name of a ducal town in Normandy) has 250 acres that are a splendid preserve of well tended lawns, gardens and natural woodlands. Since no kingdom is complete without its share of peacocks, a special circular building was designed to house them. They were free to roam about, adding a decorative touch to the vast rolling lawns.

CASTLE GOULD.

ENTRANCE TO THE STABLE

CASTLE GOULD
Nassau County Historical Museum

CASTLE GOULD

Standing high atop a cliff, a Gothic edifice rivaling that of European monarchs was commissioned by Howard Gould in 1901. Architect Abner Haydel designed a copy of Ireland's Kilkenny Castle, the ancestral home of the Marquis of Armond. Howard Gould was the son of Jay Gould, who was referred to at one time as the most hated man in America. Jay Gould made his millions by buying up Erie Railroad stock, often using violence along the way. He then went on to corner the gold market during the Grant administration. Socially ostracized, he spent twenty painful years dying of tuberculosis.

Jay Gould's son Howard married a circus performer, Katherine Clemmons. They spent their honeymoon on his 272-foot yacht, the *Niagara*, sailing abroad, where they were received by royalty throughout Europe. When they returned to New York, Howard's wife begged that a castle be built for her in Sands Point. In an awesome ability to realize their fantasies, Castle Gould was built. Inside, the main entrance hall towers up to a staggering height, from which a rusting Gothic chandelier hangs. To the left, one enters the great hall, reminiscent of an elaborate railroad station in Paris. The ceiling, like that of an all-glass palm court, was done in Tiffany-style Art Nouveau. It

CASTLE GOULD, LATER THE HOME OF DANIEL GUGGENHEIM
The Nassau County Historical Museum

was gutted out when the building was later owned by the Federal Government and used as a Naval training device center. The palm court and library was a replica of the Bromley room at South Kensington Museum in England.

In matching Gothic style were the fortress-like racing stables. One could drive through the huge arched entrance above which was a central tower that seemed to reach up to the heavens. The building was used to house the horses and grooms; coachmen occupied the quarters above. Inside one of the spacious rooms is a curious sight: a dismantled carousel, with its horses, zebras and green gaping frogs lined up against the wall as though awaiting a magic wand to bring them all back to life.

Gould lavished another million on a casino that stood near the water; a bowling alley, guest rooms and a swimming pool were built to delight his guests. He and Katherine separated in 1907 after it was rumored she ran off with the architect. In 1917, Daniel Guggenheim of copper mine fame bought the castle and renamed it Hempstead House. Also found on the property is a lordly stone carriage house that can be seen from the main road. What cannot be seen is the gilded carriage that was once

MAIN STAIRCASE
Nassau County Historical Museum

NORTH HALL. CASTLE GOULD
Nassau County Historical Museum

used for royal processions and now stands forgotten on wooden blocks. A scene from the film "The Godfather" was filmed in the building. Still another manor house is found on the estate. Mille Fleurs was built after Daniel Guggenheim died. His widow commissioned the smaller French dwelling since she felt the castle was too big for one person.

REPLICA OF A ROOM IN KENSINGTON, ENGLAND
Nassau County Historical Museum

HARBOR HILL

HARBOR HILL

I regret never having seen Harbor Hill. It was destroyed long before I ever knew it existed. It was here at Clarence H. Mackay's six-hundred-acre estate that one of the most fabulous parties ever given in American history took place in the summer of 1924. Upon arriving in this country to attend the International Polo matches between Great Britain and the United States in Old Westbury, the Prince of Wales is quoted as having said, "I am very impressed by the grand scale of hospitality on Long Island."

Grand scale indeed it was. On September 6, 1924, the handsome Prince was honored at Harbor Hill. The French château lit up the summer night sky in a blaze of light. There are some who say it could be seen glowing off in the distance from as far away as Connecticut. Thousands of blue electric lights glowed in the double rows of maple trees lining the mile-long drive, while towering high above the gabled roof were the stars and stripes of the American flag, especially made in electric lights for the gala occasion. Twelve hundred bejeweled guests, among them the most noted people of their time, included members of the British and American polo teams, ambassadors, brigadier generals, celebrities, nobility, and of course the fabulously rich Long Island set, all of whom had comparable showplaces on the Sound.

Flowers were in abundance everywhere, while guests feasted on every conceivable culinary delight including a six foot high lobster tree set on a table in the large marquee that had been built on the lawn. A famous silver set was used for the dinner. Designed by Tiffany and Co., it was made from silver from John W. Mackay's Nevada silver mines. Scenes from the pioneer days of the Golden West were depicted. On the tables there were red roses arranged in perfect order, tied with satin ribbons, and frozen by some mysterious means in the center of huge three-hundred-pound blocks of ice.

In the garden the fountains, rivaling those at Versailles, were filled with perfumed water to intoxicate the summer air, while pastel lights reflected the marble nymphs who gazed down in wonderment. Paul Whiteman and two orchestras in white tie and tails played till dawn as was the custom of the day, and there were Broadway stars to brighten the evening's entertainment. Of course, there were always those who found their way fully clothed to the bottom of the pool; footmen were on hand to fish them out and escort them upstairs to dry out.

Later, in 1927, a similar gala was given to honor Charles Lindbergh. He came to Harbor Hill in a motorcade, but, exhausted by all the festivities, he left through the back door without saying a word, leaving Clarence Mackay in a state of shock, along with his six hundred bewildered guests.

The fortune that built the Roslyn Harbor palace began with John W. Mackay, a Dublin shipyard worker who discovered the Comstock Lode, which yielded him $200,000 a month for the rest of his life. He later founded the great communications network, American Telephone & Telegraph. His son Clarence was educated in England and married Kitty Duer, to the shock of her old society family. Clarence's father built Harbor Hill as a wedding present in 1900. It was copied after the renowned French Château Maison Lafitte and built on the highest point on Long Island, where bonfires had been built during the Revolutionary War to warn of the approach of British troops.

Clarence, who spent all of his time maintaining his father's massive businesses, later lost his wife when she ran off with a handsome surgeon, Dr. Joseph Blake. Despairing over his loss, he comforted himself by adding treasures to his vast domain. The great hall, which housed a giant fireplace, contained one of the most famous collections of medieval European armor in the world. This collection was maintained by a curator from the Metropolitan Museum of Art. The oak paneled walls were hung with colorful battle and processional flags. There are four sets of old oak choir stalls along the wall from an old European cathedral.

While billiard rooms were very popular retreats for the men, no other North Shore estate could boast a 90x60-foot billiard room but Mackay's. Its oak paneled walls were decorated with mounted heads of moose, boar, deer, buffalo and antelope, that gazed down from the towering walls. Some of the other adjoining rooms were a library hung with rare tapestries and a glass palm court, with lush tropical plants and huge pots filled with mammoth Boston ferns and white wicker furniture. A graceful center fountain gave the room a dream-like effect, as it overlooked the Italian gardens. It took

HARBOR HILL

one hundred gardeners to maintain the formal gardens and grounds. There were landscaped malls and terraced gardens, and a French style rose trellis of soft blue that was fifteen feet high, built in a half moon shape eighty feet around. On each corner were two large baskets filled with fresh cut flowers.

The fabulous carriage house was as impressive in style as the main house, with its unique center peaked roof that looked like an Arabian Nights fantasy. The estate was a complete universe unto itself, with endless rows of greenhouses for scientific horticulture, a dairy farm and poultry farm, kennels for racing dogs, separate polo stables, blacksmith shops, an auto repair shop, and shops for carpentry and plumbing, charming guest houses, and a casino added in 1906 that housed the indoor pool, bowling alleys, shooting galleries, squash court, gymnasium and Turkish bath. The

167

STABLES

indoor tennis court, actually a court tennis court, is one of two on Long Island and it had its own resident tennis pro, Cecil Fairs. The estate also had its own 300,000 gallon water tower.

There are some who claim that Harbor Hill, for all its grandeur, was a bleak place. It was tainted by still another tragedy when Mackay's daughter Ellen fell in love with a poor immigrant songwriter named Irving Berlin in 1923. She married him and later had a son, but it is said that her father never spoke to her again. When her young son died on Christmas, Mackay did not attend the funeral. Clarence Mackay died in 1938 at the age of 64, following an operation for appendicitis. The big house was closed for the last time, and over the years fell to ruin. In the 'Forties a fire gutted out most of the house. The manor, stable, and casino were all destroyed to make way for small houses and the Roslyn High School.

Bill Donaldson, one of the caretakers, loved the place and knew its days would end. Through all the years of its heyday he kept a diary of clippings, recording all the social events that took place there. Those records are now part of a collection at the Bryant Library in Roslyn. Today all that is left of the estate is the rusting gates that once guarded the entrance on Roslyn Road, and a Louis XVI granite statue, "The Horse Tamer," just northeast of where it once stood in the formal garden, now the Roslyn High School courtyard.

ORMSTON HOUSE

Though John E. Aldred was born in Lawrence, Massachusetts of poor parents, by the time he was sixty he had accumulated $80,000,000 from his Gillette Safety Razor Company, Consolidated Gas Company of New York, and from foreign investments. It was in 1910 that Aldred, and his equally wealthy friend W. D. Guthrie bought themselves the town of Lattingtown. They had sixty homes and stores leveled to make way for their palatial residences. It took six years to complete the Gothic and Tudor style mansion, which contained some forty rooms. As was the trend in this fabled day, most of the materials for the house and furniture and even the trees for the garden were brought from abroad. Aldred got his architect, Henry W. Rowe, to design an imitation of an English country manor. The feudal splendor of the main floor is enhanced by the oak beamed ceilings and leaded glass windows with stained glass insets, brought from England. The flagstone floors came from an ancient English castle, and

A FOUNTAIN IN THE GARDEN

the wood for the great dining hall was proudly hauled from Sherwood Forest.

The main floor contained a fabulous built-in pipe organ, and a variety of imported fireplaces. There are also the usual living room, main dining room, drawing room, library, and breakfast room. In the east wing are found the kitchens, service rooms and pantries. Upstairs there are thirteen master bedrooms with ten tiled baths and another thirteen servants' rooms. Outside, Ormston House has two of the most picturesque gate houses, one at the east end of the estate, the other at the west end entrance, which is guarded by a breathtaking iron gate designed by Samuel Yellin of

LEAD STATUE IN THE GARDEN

STONE PAVILION

GRAND HALL PANELING CONCEALS THE TWO-STORY CATHEDRAL PIPE ORGAN

LOGGIA, ORMSTON HOUSE

Philadelphia. Also on the grounds are the stables and garage, with a coach room containing an antique English Tally-ho.

Alongside the two outdoor tennis courts that face the Sound are two more guest houses hidden amongst the trees. A classic style tea and bath house overlook the 1,400 feet of private beach on the Sound. The wooden dock that once extended from the bathhouse has long since fallen into the sea, as the little house is also falling to ruin—a dramatic sight against the setting sun.

In 1916, when Ormston was completed, the cost to Mr. Aldred was $3,000,000. Another $500,000 was spent on appropriate furnishings and then another $200,000 to landscape the 119 acres of gardens. As one might expect, some forty-seven servants were required to run and maintain the house, at an additional cost of $100,000 a year. Besides the butler and housekeeper there were fifteen other house servants, the master's valet, a personal maid for Mrs. Aldred, two footmen, the "Cordon Bleu Chef," who kept a constant supply of out-of-season delicacies, a seamstress, two chamber maids, a laundress, and one downstairs maid. On the surrounding grounds there were the two watchmen, the superintendent, the gatekeepers, three chauffeurs, two grooms, dairy and cattle hands, a mechanic, groundskeepers and head gardener, a tree expert, and handymen to pluck the weeds. Aldred and his wife lived as Lord Baron and Baroness until a business error caused him to lose his fortune. Ormston was sold in 1957 for a mere $75,000 to an order of Ukranian monks who use it as a monastery.

ZOG RUINS

Just off the recently widened Highway 106 in Syosset, there lie the toppled remains of Knollwood. In grim haunted desolation the once stately columns, fountains and fragments of ornate carvings converge together in a twisted, broken, shattered mass, surrounded still by a balustraded terrace that once outlined the entire house. Those ruins and crumbling foundation flanked by massive steps leading to the lower garden are all that is left of the former regal home of King Zog, the exiled King of Albania. The sixty-two-room classic mansion, built originally by Charles Mc Veigh, a New York lawyer, once stood on a hill that overlooked 267 acres of extensive landscaping, gardens, and reflecting pools. The house, with its wide terraces, Ionic columns, and Romanesque

173

COLONNADE

summer houses of stone and marble, was nestled amidst a half-mile circle of rhododendron bushes.

It was in 1951 that the Long Island showplace received national attention when King Zog the First, a feudal mountain fighter, and last monarch of his country, came to the North Shore in search of a place to settle his small kingdom. He bought Knollwood, supposedly paying for the mansion with a bucket full of diamonds and rubies. Zog, with his love for highly decorated uniforms, boasted a colorful life, but in truth fate had dealt cruelly with him. At the age of seventeen he assumed the post of chief of one of Albania's mountain clan tribes. It was sixteen years later that he was crowned king in 1928. Legend has it that Zog sought the crown in order to revenge himself against the father of his first love. The story has it that not only was Zog's suit for the girl's hand in marriage rejected, but the father, chieftain of a rival tribe, killed his daughter and sent the girl's body to Zog as a wedding present. As king, Zog was further tormented by a series of attempted assassinations and in 1939 Mussolini took over the small country. Zog narrowly escaped death by crossing the border just in time.

After many years of waiting to win back his country, Zog gave up all hope and came to America. As news spread to the North Shore socialites, who were eager to be the first to receive him in the usual grand manner, welcomers gathered around the imposing wrought iron gates, only to be met by a strange bearded figure in Czarist Russian army uniform, who, after kissing the visitors' hands would promptly turn them away. While all awaited the arrival of Zog and his Queen Geraldine, for some mysterious reason he never moved into his estate, nor did his expected busloads of Albanian subjects. It was announced in 1954 by one of King Zog's attorneys that the king would set up a kingdom on the estate and would leave parcels of land to his subjects who would work the land as tenants.

As years passed with no sign of the notorious king, tax difficulties began to mount. Though Zog had announced he would claim sovereign immunity as a foreign

king, county officials thought differently, and preparations were made to sell the estate. With the sudden disappearance of the bearded gatekeeper, the estate was left unguarded and was soon besieged by vandals in search of treasures that were rumored to be buried on the grounds. No trace of them was found, just as no trace had been found of the mysterious king, and in 1959 the long empty mansion was demolished, leaving only the restless ivy to cover the wounds of a forgotten dream.

RUINS OF STAIRS TO GARDEN

THE ORIGINAL LIBRARY

CLAYTON

Charles Frick

Lloyd Bryce, a distinguished author of the late 19th century, originally built Clayton in 1904. The imposing Georgian brick manor house was originally designed by Ogden Codman, Jr. and built on a point giving it a picturesque open view of Hempstead Harbor. In 1917 the estate was bought by Charles Frick, son of Henry Clay Frick, one of the founders of U.S. Steel. His New York home and art collection are now the Frick Museum. Frick set about with his own architect, Charles Carrick Allom of London, to redesign the front façade and make major alterations to the house's interior.

The rose colored brick was laid in Flemish bond, and has a low hipped roof with a wooden balustrade running along most of the top. A loggia connects the north and south wing identical projections, that are softened by clinging ivy. All the ground floor windows are of the Venetian arched style except for the west front. The grounds include five miles of bridle paths; at one time a ski slope; polo field; two tennis courts,

THE ORIGINAL DRAWING ROOM

one grass, the other clay; a lake; and an animal village, one of the few on Long Island. A special arborist from Austria was brought over to supervise the planting of the "pinetum," which included 190 species of rare trees.

The formal garden, though now untended, is dominated by an all-teak treillage. A central semi-circular arbor is topped by a dome which rises some 25 feet from a pair of lattice columns. Though faded and covered by grapevines, its Chinese style fretwork recalls the gardens of Versailles. In the 'Thirties, Mrs. Frick commissioned several prominent landscape architects to design the complex scrollwork laid out in gravel. At one time a bronze fountain of dolphins at play stood in the small reflecting pool in the center of the rose garden. To the west was the azalea garden and east a garden lush with summer blossoms of every color. After the death of Mrs. Frick in 1953, the entire landscape arrangement was simplified.

The interior of the main house was lavish in style and the main entrance hall had highly polished marble floors and rich oak paneling. A winding staircase with turned balusters that reached up to the third floor formed an oval. Fluted Corinthian oak columns divide the entrance hall from its flanking antechambers. Just off the staircase is the library, now empty, and a vestibule leading to a circular colonnade with apse-like alcoves. The main drawing room is lined with pine paneling imported from England along with the parquet floors. The room is an ideal setting for the music recitals that are given there during the summer months. The upstairs bedrooms, all with separate baths, were decorated in the feminine style of the day. The most impressive room was the master bedroom chamber with its delicate chinoiserie wallpaper of floral sprays and

THE SOUTH WING

exotic birds and butterflies.

Also located on the property is a historic Gothic Revival house built by the poet William Cullen Bryant in 1860. Plans are now being made to restore its all but vine-covered exterior. In 1969 Clayton, with its remaining 165 acres, was purchased by Nassau County and is presently used as the Nassau County Center for the Fine Arts.

FRONT FAÇADE

TEMPLETON

Reflected in the waters of a tranquil lake stands Templeton, a neo-classic Georgian manor house considered to be one of the most palatial of the North Shore residences. Built originally by the Dupont family in 1920, it was later bought by steel magnate Winston F. C. Guest, who was a third cousin of the late Winston Churchill. Guest came from an old-line socialite family and was ranked as one of the top polo players in the world. His first wife was F. W. Woolworth's daughter Helena Mc Cann. They were divorced in 1944, and he later married the beautiful Lucy Douglas Cochrane in 1947. Mrs. Guest, an aristocratic woman with great style and taste, was of the manor born. Many times voted the best dressed woman in the world, she is now listed in the Fashion Hall of Fame. Local residents often recall seeing her galloping her fine thoroughbred horses across the open meadows.

ENTRANCE GATES TO THE ENCLOSED GARDEN

    Templeton, encompassing 130 acres, represents the results of an architect's goal to combine grace and refinement in its surroundings. The house fits perfectly into its setting, the grounds are simple with sweeping vistas and grassy slopes. A marble balustrade graced with classic marble urns runs along the west, north and east sides of the stately mansion. The east façade is an architectural triumph; perched on a marble terraced slope it faces a wide lawn dotted with pine trees. The main east pavilion is centered above a flight of marble stairs and is the most elaborately decorated section of the edifice. Massive limestone pillars support an open loggia flanking the house in a semicircle, terminated with an open brick archway. Over the main center door is an

GATES TO THE ENCLOSED GARDEN

elaborately designed relief: its fanciful trim is embellished by an urn set into an oval recessed niche.

As you approach the entrance courtyard there are high brick walls softened by linden trees; two wrought iron gates mark the entrance to an enclosed garden, now overgrown. Built into a walled in terrace on the north side of the garden is an unusual keyhole-shaped swimming pool where water flows from three marble shells. A long winding road ends with a bleak reminder of the 20th century—a housing development occupies the site of the once-active and rambling wood frame stable where the guests once housed their riding horses. When the famous Lipizzan horses from the Spanish riding school of Austria came to New York to perform at Madison Square Garden, Mrs. C. Z. Guest offered that they be her guests at her spacious polo stables. Perhaps the most impressive feature of the house is the grand white marble staircase with its elaborate cornices and carved newel posts and balusters. Most of the spacious rooms were characteristic of a trend in the 'Twenties when owners sought to recapture the refinement and splendor of European country houses.

To the right is the oak paneled ballroom, now empty. I recall one night in 1977 when it was brought back to life for a black tie charity ball to raise funds for Long Island's TV station, Channel 21. The light reflecting from the candles through the open French doors onto the waltzing guests in their tuxedos and flowing gowns did create a magical mood. Just to the left of the center hall is the library, whose walls were once lined with a collection of rare books. At one end of the room stood a carved rosewood Louis XVI desk. Lending color were the rich emerald green velvet draperies and chairs.

The focal point of the dining room was a series of handsomely framed family portraits covering four generations: one of Mrs. Frederick Guest was painted by John Singer Sargent. Also in the room was a copy of a painting of Mrs. Henry Phipps. The original is in her former home, now the famous Old Westbury Gardens. Mrs. Guest had

THE SITTING ROOM

one of the finest collections of Chinese porcelains. Many of them were displayed in tiny little niches in the oak room, which was accented by tall fluted panels and carved cornices.

THE MARBLE STAIR HALL

UPSTAIRS BALCONY, STAIR HALL

In 1966, while it was still privately owned, the house was opened to the public for a fund raising. Unexpected crowds attended, and Mrs. Guest soon ordered the main road blocked, when cars began parking on the front lawn, ruining the grass. Still another crowd filled the halls in 1968 when movie crews took over to film some scenes from the movie "A New Leaf." To save wear and tear on a valuable fifty-foot Aubusson rug, ingenious set designers made a copy of the rug painted on heavy plain canvas. On camera it looked as good as the original.

Today Templeton is a grey reflection of its former splendor. It is now owned by New York Technical University and, like so many of the estates, is being used as a conference center.

MAIN ENTRANCE FACING NORTH

RYEFIELD MANOR

A wide four-acre manicured lawn sets off Ryefield Manor, a fine example of Georgian architecture. It was built in 1915 by shipping magnate George Carver. In spring the red brick and white trim walls set off the colorful azalea and dogwood trees that surround the house. While the exterior is simple, with four classic Ionic pillars reaching up to a wood and stucco pediment, it is the eclectic style of the interiors that makes the house outstanding.

THE LOUIS XVI SITTING ROOM

Inside, a magnificent oak paneled reception hall towers up three stories to a vaulted stained glass ceiling. To the left is the main staircase with a thick red silk draped cord railing held in place by iron loops secured to the wall. A carved wood balcony is built around three sides of the hall. Tapestries, armorials and torchères give the room a sixteenth century feudal look. Despite all the dark wood paneling and marble, the house has an inviting warmth to it. Many of the rooms are of different periods and styles. To

LOUNGE

the left of the main door entrance is a dark green morning room with ornate gilded mouldings and cornices, and French period furnishings.

One passes a small study to the right, just before entering the dining room, which is formal with stately proportions and exquisite furnishings. A gilt filigree oval mirror reflects an ethereal 18th century crystal chandelier that hangs over the mahogany table in the center of the room. The library is reached through another dark wood vestibule on the right of the hall. Rich paneled bookshelves cover four sides of the room. The main feature is the simple mantel with a center niche and flanked by fluted panels. Also on the main floor is a solarium with a tiled ceramic floor, and a classic wall fountain surrounded by ferns and other plants. The walls are lattice wood over a silver and leaf design wall paper. The original Victorian wicker furnishings have since been replaced with more modern garden furniture.

Just before one reaches the second floor through a high corniced arch one finds an elegant mezzanine drawing room flooded by light from wide leaded glass windows. These windows, which surround the wing on three sides, are embellished with insets of imported stained glass. The sunny room is dominated by two mammoth exotic Solium plants that span some fourteen feet across. The kitchens and pantries are located in the east wing along with the servants' quarters that once accommodated the fourteen servants it took to run the house. The main kitchen is long and narrow and retains much of its old-fashioned charm, with its tiled walls and original oak cabinets and drawers; white ceramic plaques are used as labels to keep the kitchen supplies in order.

The rear garden pool area is simple in design and moderate in scale. Originally, a long reflecting pool ran the width of the walled-in garden, but it has since been replaced by a handsome swimming pool set off by two classic stone urns. Opening off the spacious living room on the main floor is a pillared loggia or open porch, all but obscured by the pine trees growing around it. Though the 30-room house has changed owners four times in the past seven years, it has been completely restored and enjoyed very much as in the old days by its new and proud owners.

RYEFIELD, MASTER BEDROOM

THE PAVILLION

DARK HOLLOW

THE MAIN LIVING ROOM TODAY

Dark Hollow is one of the North Shore's most splendid survivors, an architectural gem designed by Danish-born Mons Tvede and Mott Schmidt in 1930. It was built by Walter Jennings, who was then chairman of the board of Standard Oil, and was given to his son Oliver Jennings for a wedding present. Taking its inspiration from a palace in Leningrad that was once owned by Prince Youssipov, the man who is said to have killed Rasputin, the Danish neo-Classic Palladian Villa was built above a three-hundred-foot-long sea wall commanding a spectacular view of the Sound. Even today it is still a very liveable house, with magnificent proportions, and recalls a colorful and romantic past.

It was Mrs. Isa Jennings, the statuesque South American beauty, who gave the legendary parties at the Long Island showplace. Cole Porter, Baron Alexis De Rede, Mrs. Hugh Auchincloss, Princess Chavchavodye, who brought the alleged Anastasia, the only survivor from the Russian royal family, to America, were among the many who visited Dark Hollows. Lavish Spanish costume parties were staged by Isa, who flew bands and flamenco combos up from Latin America to add to the festivities. Considered to be an authority on the circus, she made the fashion pages in her colorful and unusual outfits she designed herself. Guests often came by private yacht and docked along the long wooden pier aglow with lanterns strung along the railing for the occasion, while the sea wall was ablaze with dozens of flaming torches.

At one end of the sea wall is an outstanding white classic pavilion with copper domed roof oxidized to a turquoise shade and graced at the top by a marble urn. Inside, set into the wall, is an ancient marble Renaissance altar with winged angels, brought from a chapel in Florence. The pavilion is open to gentle breezes by way of four high whitewashed arches with louvered shutters that open out to the Sound. The North Shore had a fondness for these secluded circular temples that were once the havens of queens, who took afternoon tea there as they exchanged ideas with their philosophers. Often hidden away in some secret corner of the garden amidst ivory blossoms and the perfume of honeysuckle, they were a place to dream away the afternoon and be entertained by the gentle hum of bees and long low call of passing sea gulls.

For the romantic at heart, they were the haunts of lovers who might sit hand in hand on ruffled chintz and rattan chairs and exchange stolen kisses while watching the sea and stars on a moonlit night. Mrs. Jennings served cocktails in her outdoor pavilion as guests arrived on their luxurious yachts. I am told she was a believer in the occult and often spent many long afternoons in quiet meditation there.

Dark Hollow is hidden away in a thicket of woods at the bottom of a steep mile-long winding drive terminated by an open central arch that leads into a courtyard. Stone obelisk shapes and bronze urns flank the entrance on either side of the white stucco carriage house that faces the villa. One enters the house through glass French doors that open onto a rotunda that soars up forty-five feet to a glass starburst design skylight. At the second floor landing a wrought iron railing runs full circle around a balcony. Originally all the floors on the main floor were glazed Della Robbia blue with a brass-outlined mandala in the entrance hall.

The main living room was a reflection of Mrs. Jennings' exquisite taste; the entire house was confined to a blue and white color scheme, even to the massive awnings that shade the 30-foot Palladian window. The domed ceiling in the living room towered up

ORIGINAL MASTER BEDROOM

to 42 feet and was painted a pale blue; a gilded Greek key border with indirect cove lighting gave the room an ethereal quality. The room was eclectic in style and way ahead of its time—sumptuously furnished with fine Chippendale pieces, comfortable chairs, and a huge Corinthian pillar capital piece served as a coffee table. Several rare Wedgwood urns adorned the simple mantel with its matching center plaque. Mrs. Isa Jennings, a noted connoisseur of the arts, filled the bedroom with treasures she had found in Europe. A pair of Peking carved wooden and lacquered arm chairs were placed on either side of Louis XV chinoiserie lacquer cabinet with gilt stand that dominated one wall. Leopard skins covered the bed and were reflected in a mirrored wall with mirrored display cases filled with Ming and other Oriental vases surrounding a simple fireplace.

There is an extraordinary similarity between the late Mrs. Oliver Jennings and the new owner, Ivory Tower, a dark-haired beauty with doe-like eyes who bought the house in 1970. They both loved the arts and collecting rare exotic treasures from all parts of Europe and the Far East. Much of the flavor of the place has been maintained and enhanced by Ivory, who has replaced the original blue floors that were beginning to crack from age, with white Carrara marble floors throughout the first floor. The main room is breathtaking: no camera has yet captured its essence. Four twenty-foot ficus trees cast filigreed shadows on the all-white walls. The sofas are done in all white, as are the two splendid Venetian grotto chairs that came from Helena Rubenstein's Paris apartment. Color is provided by vibrant Moroccan rugs scattered about the floors.

A wall of handsome twenty-foot bookcases set into three windowed alcoves is graced by a pair of silver gilt Chinese Chippendale mirrors that hang on the two outer walls. The main features of the room are two twenty-foot paintings done by Paul Jenkins that hang on opposite walls. In one corner of the room is an original painting by Monticelli that once hung in the bedroom of the William Woodward house in Oyster Bay. It was in the room at his untimely death in 1955. On either side of the huge window that overlooks the Sound is a pair of wrought iron torchères that once belonged to Thomas Costain, author of *The Silver Chalice*. Everywhere there are colorful paintings done by David Burliuk, ceramics done by Picasso, and works by other well-known artists. In the entrance rotunda, one is greeted by the outstretched hands of a seventeenth-century Kuan Yin Bodhisattva seated in a lotus blossom set on a lacquer stand. This Buddha is an old Indian bronze image of the eleven-faced, thousand-armed Avalokitesvara, redeemer of hell. In each palm there is an eye, each of which signifies some power; the sun and moon were to illuminate man from darkness; and the bottle at one time contained medicine to cure illness.

There is so much to behold it would be impossible to list all the objects of interest and their history. The master bathroom is especially interesting with its cobalt blue glazed tub sunk into a mirrored niche that reflects many fine oriental blue and white bowls and a silver gilt chair in the shape of a stylized hand, done by the well-known artist Pedro. A marble wash basin in the shape of a shell is set with hand-painted blue porcelain faucets. Overhead is a whimsical chandelier of painted wrought iron flowers, birds, and butterflies. For the 'Seventies, a new look has been given to the master bedroom which is simply decorated with a fabulous sixteenth century Ming Dynasty red lacquer four poster bed, covered with exquisite sheets of linen with sprays of pink dogwood branches.

The upstairs guest bedrooms are cool and dignified with French doors opening out to the sea-view balconies. In one, there stands a white bamboo canopied bed with sumptuous blue and white ruffled draperies tied back with silk Chinese tassels. The walls are a vivid cobalt blue, the only exception in the house to the all-white color scheme. A Picasso print hangs over the mantel that supports several Oriental vases. Hundreds of paintings by Burliuk line the walls of a long gallery that stretches from one end of the second floor to the other. Another recent addition to the estate is the magnificent pool set above the eight-foot-thick sea wall just above the Sound, that was designed to curve around a tree and rock garden containing a Japanese flowering plum tree. Today the house is often seen in the pages of *Vogue* and *Harpers Bazaar*, as cosmetic companies and fashion houses vie to capture what is probably the most remarkable house on the East Coast.

MING DYNASTY BED IN THE PRESENT MASTER BEDROOM

A SECTION OF THE
ENTRANCE ROTUNDA

MASTER BATHROOM

MAIN ENTRANCE, BEFORE THE FIRE

SIR ASHLEY SPARKS ESTATE

Rows of chestnut trees line the mile-long drive which once led to the Ashley Sparks mansion. Standing at the top of a sweeping hill, the forty-two-room house reminds one of many Southern plantations. The front of the house was supported by four lofty columns in the classic tradition, and is flanked by treillage obscured by overgrown masses of wisteria. Sir Ashley Sparks was the flamboyant chairman of the board of the

AFTER THE FIRE

RUINS

HOUSE FACING THE GARDENS AND SWIMMING POOL

Cunard Steamship line, and started the house sometime before the 'Twenties and kept adding wings and extensions. The Stone Room, as it was called, was used as a reception and entertaining room. It was set off by a huge rustic stone fireplace, with stuffed animal heads above it. A glassed-in terrace and sun porch was supported by four Ionic columns. A library of dark oak-paneled walls overlooked the formal columns and pool.

Outside, on the three-hundred-acre estate are found dogwood, spruce and Japanese cherry, and magnolia trees. A breathtaking view of the Sound could be seen from the second floor bedrooms. Typical of Gold Coast life, the manor was the setting for many parties, including a garden wedding for Sir Ashley's daughter. Since the death of Mr. Sparks in 1963, the house had been empty, invaded by vandals who have destroyed its beauty and elegance. Vandals presumably set the fire in the spring of 1970, and what remained of the house was finally bulldozed. Only the rambling stables remain standing, though the chemistry of time has taken its toll there too and this estate, like many others, is doomed to become the site of some modern development.

ENTRANCE TO THE VANDERBILT ESTATE

WILLIAM K. VANDERBILT

The former summer home of William K. Vanderbilt stands on the top of a hill overlooking picturesque Northport Harbor. Now open to the public as a museum, it

THE VANDERBILT MARINE MUSEUM

contains a unique, and one of the most complete private collections of marine life. For over thirty years Mr. Vanderbilt set out on his scientific expeditions aboard his two-hundred-and-fifty-foot yacht, the *Alva*. His private collection of over 17,000 varieties of marine specimens displayed in natural habitat settings is housed in a huge Spanish Moroccan building patterned after the main house.

At the main entrance one passes several columns from the ancient ruins of Carthage, which now stand atop a vista overlooking the harbor. A cobblestone drive crosses a bridge to reveal a massive stone archway enlivened by a decorative belltower, and ancient tower clock. Beyond the medieval gates lies the center courtyard paved with Belgian blocks. The interiors of the twenty-four-room mansion are furnished with numerous antiques and exotic works of art. A massive room on the lower level of the main house displays several unusual marine life habitat exhibits: blue lights give the impression of being under water as they are set under a transparent glass floor.

THE REFLECTING POOL

A long narrow dining room of Spanish Moroccan style was carefully reconstructed with tiled floor, carved wooden ceiling, and rough plaster walls, and graced with antique Moorish weapons that are inlaid with silver, ivory, and jewels. A set of Renaissance side chairs surround an eleven-foot Florentine seventeenth century refectory table of carved walnut. The room's main feature is a corner fireplace with the Vanderbilt coat of arms painted on it.

One of the most opulent rooms in the mansion is the organ room—rich with the warm glow of oak paneling. A $90,000 pipe organ is concealed behind an 18th century Aubusson Chinoiserie tapestry. An ornate Caun mantel and fireplace dominate the room. Mrs. Vanderbilt's bedroom and dressing room reflect the Louis XVI period. The bathtub is of a solid block of black marble, set with fixtures of solid gold. The original French furnishings have been replaced with a collection of trophies of the founder, Commodore Cornelius Vanderbilt. Further down the long hallway is Mr. Vanderbilt's room, of the Empire style.

The forty-acre estate grounds are carefully preserved. This is one of the best examples of Gold Coast life. The estate has been open to the public since 1950, and the institution is being supported by a legacy from William K. Vanderbilt. It is now administered by the Board of Trustees of the Suffolk County Park Commission.

REMAINS OF THE AVIARY, FORMER HOME OF HUNDREDS OF RARE EXOTIC BIRDS

LAURALTON HALL

Lewis C. Tiffany

Lauralton Hall, the eighty-five-room mansion designed by Lewis C. Tiffany, was completed in 1905, and was considered one of the showplaces of the century. The steel frame, brick and stucco house was asymmetrical in style, and set off dramatically by huge stained glass windows that gave the rooms a daring theatrical feeling. A small

THE MAIN ENTRANCE IS GUARDED BY TWO CELADON FOO DOGS
Heckscher Museum

stream ran through the center of the enclosed court that contained an unusual clear glass fountain.

Without the aid of an architect, Tiffany worked out the plans for the house in clay. He included many Art Nouveau forms with Islamic overtones. The Mission Moorish influence found throughout was said to be unlike anything ever done before or since. The main entrance to the house was set behind four concrete columns, with floral capitals decorated with glass mosaics. Between each of the columns hung glass Tiffany lanterns and Kang Hsi lions of glazed turquoise blue guarded this unique entrance. Tiffany's magnificent imagination inspired him to design a variety of stained glass windows made in 1885, for the dimly lit living room: some of the subjects were flowers, fish, fruit, the feeding of the flamingoes, the four seasons, and the bathers in the dream garden. Outside, a giant rock crystal in a round pool served as a centerpiece for a stream. The landscape centered around informal gardens of wisteria, and exotic tropical plants.

Inside, the dining room ran the full length of the house, with clear glass panes shedding light on the tiled floor. Tiffany's famous wisteria glass works enclosed a veranda at the west end. In 1957 a mysterious fire consumed the famed mansion, taking with it what was then considered the most important achievement of Art Nouveau architecture in America. All that remains of the former home of L. C. Tiffany is a small stone chapel originally made for the Chicago World's Fair in 1893, and what appears to be the charred remains of an enormous glass palm court, which was used as a passage from the main house to the greenhouse.

RUINS OF DOORWAY
TO A CHAPEL, 1966

IRON GRILLE FACING EAST LOGGIA

LA SALVA

Frederick Wheeler Estate

A beautiful example of Italian Renaissance architecture is found in the classic lines of
the former Frederick Wheeler estate. It was built in 1918 by Henry Sanderson, Esq.   207

REAR FACADE FACING THE GREAT LAWN

The forty-room mansion was bought by Mr. Wheeler in 1927. Sheltered under its terra cotta tiled roof are Renaissance and Byzantine interiors that range in style from the fifteenth century to the eighteenth. The spacious loggias that overlook poetic gardens were designed to accommodate splendid doors and wrought iron works imported from England.

In the dining room were a pair of hand-carved 15th century Italian oak doors depicting mythological scenes, armorials, griffins and lions. When a duplicate pair had to be made to balance the room, Italian artisans were brought over and paid twenty-five cents a day plus room and board. It took them several months to complete the job before they were returned home. The floor in the dining room is dark Lavento marble, and built into the upper walls are painted panels from a palace in Florence. Just off the dining room is an unusual morning room with an ornate plaster relief vaulted ceiling. Many of the furnishings were of the Roman and Egyptian periods.

There is Travertine marble throughtout the house. Many of the craftsmen, stonecutters, plasterers and woodworkers were imported to supplement local talent. The wide Byzantine style circular staircase rose to the second floor. It terminated in a dome-shaped point with a round skylight in the center, from which a heavy chandelier hung from a four-sided bracket. Originally a tapestry dating back to 1496 hung along the stairway wall, and a pair of paintings taken from a palace in Florence graced the dining room, set in recesses in the walls on each side of the fireplace. When prohibition hit, a secret wall was built to conceal the chamber where six truckloads of liquor were hidden.

The grounds were landscaped by Olmsted, who also did Central Park in Manhattan, Prospect Park in Brooklyn, and Planting Fields across the street in Oyster Bay. The Italian gardens are magnificent. One vista leads from the south terrace to the

THE LOGGIA, SOUTH WING

THE GRAND STAIRWAY

Roman Cirque garden, a wide circle of stone columns that surround a pool. A walled Italian herb garden contained massive flower beds to keep the house filled with fragrant bouquets. Grounds were planted so that flowers would only bloom during the 3 spring months that the Wheeler family lived there. Their fourteen house servants traveled with them when they stayed at their other estates and their town house in New York.

Though the house was used only three months out of the year, it was the setting for many formal garden parties. Gardens were ablaze with colorful orange, red and

ORIGINAL FURNITURE IN DINING HALL

pink azalea bushes, dogwood trees, and 20,000 daffodils that were planted along one sloping lawn. Some 200 vases of flowers were changed each day throughout the house. A full staff of servants was kept on hand all year to keep things in order. For forty years the house silently witnessed the comings and goings of family routine, but it all came to an end in 1960 when the estate was taken over by a monastery. Its now-cloistered beauty remains hidden behind a ten-foot-high stone wall and is never seen by the public.

THE LOGGIA

OAK KNOLL

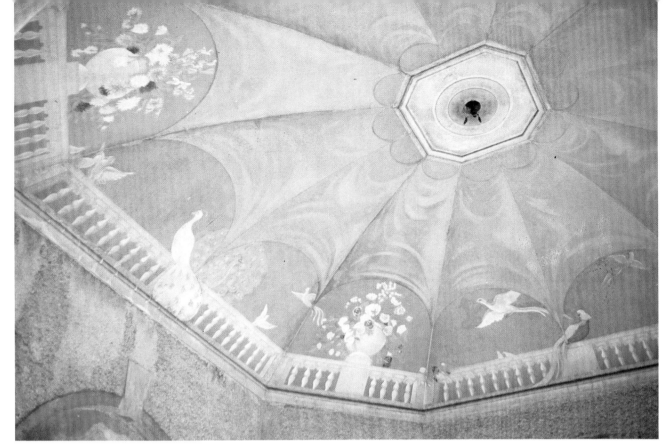

FRESCOED CEILING IN THE GAZEBO

THE COBBLESTONED ENTRANCE WAY

THE LINDEN ALLEE FROM THE GAZEBO

ENTRANCE COURTYARD

Oak Knoll is named after one of the largest oak trees on Long Island, standing in the garden of the manor house, which was built in 1916 for Bertram Work. The residence, of classic Italian style, and designed by William A. Delano, stands upon the highest point of Shore Drive in Oyster Bay. An imposing Roman style entrance with iron gates leads to a winding driveway banked with laurel. At the top of the landing is an outstanding cobblestone courtyard surrounded by rows of clipped yellow cypress, facing the reflecting pool. There are also boxwood plantings. A sweeping vista emphasizes the front façade of the villa. A strap ornamental design of limestone adorns the top of the entrance.

Inside, there are long vistas set off by rich tapestries, heavy furniture, and many stately old Italian objets d'art. The great hall, with its intricate plaster work ceiling, is typical of the Adam style; two paintings by N. C. Wyeth are hung there, along with numerous works by famous Dutch masters. An oak paneled library and walnut paneled drawing room look out over spacious lawns, classic gardens and a magnificent view of Oyster Bay Harbor. The dining room with its paneled wall paintings is typical of Gold Coast splendor.

Another room of interest is the breakfast room, with its walls decorated by Gardner Hale with unique frescoes of exotic birds, animals, and vegetation. The classic gardens are representative of the house, with statuary placed along the borders, as it would be in the old gardens of Europe. The Roman style wall garden reflects the charms of the pergola. Light and shade play in delightful patterns on the tiled floor. Oak Knoll, which was owned since the 'Thirties by the late Mrs. Joel Ellis Fisher, is presently being restored by its new owners.

THE FORMAL DINING ROOM

THE LIVING ROOM

ITALIAN FRESCO, THE BREAKFAST ROOM

THE LIBRARY

A GUEST BEDROOM

WEST FACADE

THE DRUID RUINS

ROSEMARY FARM

The Last Gold Coast Ruin

When work on this book first began sometime in the early 'Sixties, there were at least a hundred fascinating mansion ruins, abandoned and doomed, along the shores of Long Island Sound. Today there remains but one.

A faded greeting card found amid the attic clutter bears the ironic legend: "Here's Rosemary, that's for remembrance." Over those words is painted a sprig of the herb. Each year the same card was sent to hundreds of friends during the holidays. Today the house stands empty, forgotten, at the end of a lonely overgrown drive. The original wrought-iron gate, now engulfed by weeds, has been chained and padlocked for over forty years.

In 1902 Roland Conklin bought some two hundred acres in West Neck and commissioned architect Wilson Eyre to build him a great English manor house high on a bluff overlooking the sound. It is unique among North Shore houses with its double gables, overhanging bays, and grouping of richly carved windows stained a deep mahogany color. The upper walls are covered with rare shingle-type terra-cotta tile. Originally the shutters were painted a deep forest green; few remain and those that do hang at odd angles on rusting hinges. Inside the now derelict building, vines creep into many corners, reaching in through broken windows, and struggle to escape through holes in the walls. Blackbirds rustle in nests built in the exposed beams and rafters surveying the realm of musty disarray. There is an overpowering smell of arsenic (perhaps used for rat poison) filling the underground tunnel that runs from the woods to the basement of the house.

The ceilings seem on the verge of collapse, and the discolored walls are festooned with cobwebs. At one time the interiors were among the finest on the island, with unusual carvings by Edouard Meane along the main floor gallery. A pair of medieval style figures grace the stairway newel posts. Stairs that rise up to the carved gallery overlook the entire living room, where fine old paintings once hung. The master suite, with its exposed beams and colorful ceiling murals depicting the "Canterbury Tales," was imported, along with a large centuries-old stained glass window built into the far end of the room.

On the main floor an elaborately painted organ panel extends down to the floor below. Bronze lanterns hang from ancient carved beams, and a huge open fireplace stands empty. The eye is drawn to a pair of dramatic, richly carved sixteenth-century pillars that mark the entrance from the dining room to a summer porch that extends out into the rear garden.

THE REMAINS OF THE GROTTO BY THE STAGE OF THE AMPHITHEATER

THE TOWER OF THE CARRIAGE HOUSE AND STABLES

Conklin, who made and lost several fortunes in utilities, foreign transportation, and sugar, had married the beautiful Mary MacFadden in 1895. Her portrait was painted by the noted photographer and artist Edward Steichen just after Rosemary Farm was built. It hung in the main gallery until the house was closed in 1924. For winter entertaining Mr. Conklin had a huge indoor theater built in the east wing of the house. Here his and his wife's love of music was expressed as whole orchestras were brought in to perform their favorite classics. The master of the house was something of a scholar who spent much of his time in his vast Cuban mahogany paneled library. His quest for knowledge was boundless, and he often read late into the night on such subjects as the arts, Shakespeare, geology, and ancient history and its mysteries and rituals.

A short distance from the house to the north is an imposing and unusual carriage house and barn. A clock tower rises up from one side and is dominated by a pair of carved rampant dragons supporting an ancient clock.

Little remains of what was regarded as Rosemary Farm's crowning glory, a spectacular open-air amphitheater laid out in a series of multilevel stonework tiers somewhat akin to Rome's Colosseum. It was built to hold five thousand people. In its center at the lowest level, an island rose up from an artificial lake. This in turn was surrounded by intricate waterfalls, a stone bridge, and fossil coral grottoes. The island was used as the stage and was encircled by a steel pipe. When the actors needed a costume change, or the stage set replaced by another, the fountains were turned on and jets of water rose sixteen feet into the air to act as a curtain. Swans and gondolas glided about the island during intermission. There was a wide variety of performances given over the years, including a Shakespeare festival, Greek plays, and Broadway shows, with such theater greats as John and Ethel Barrymore, Tyrone Power, and Clifton Webb; for one fund raiser given for the Red Cross, John Philio Sousa performed with his two-hundred-fifty-piece band.

Surrounding this colossal structure was a dramatic view of Long Island Sound, and parklike vistas dotted with curious marble mythological creatures, including cloven-hoofed nymphs, Pan, and a statue of Sappho. Here they linger still, buried amid the tendrils of ivy that engulf the ruins today. It creeps and stretches down along the rocks and gullies, and along the floor of the now empty pool. Great wooden pillars rise up from the island, while those that have fallen lay in heaps, crushed by falling branches from the ancient trees. Other forms of vegetation struggle for space in the now choked wilderness that was once the theater.

At the base of a steep drop in the contour of the land are what some refer to as the Druid ruins. No one knows what their exact purpose was, although they make a compelling sight as the light filtering through the trees cast an eerie glow on the series of wide stone arches. It is believed that Conklin collected many of the stone boulders from ancient ruins on his world travels. Some are millions of years old and are said to have been transported from Incan and Mayan temples, and the area around Stonehenge in England. These were incorporated into the design of the structure along with local stones as well. At the center is a large basin or well now filled with murky, stagnant water.

BLACKTON'S BOATHOUSE

It was the kind of ruin that when you sailed through Cold Spring Harbor, you couldn't help but wonder what it must have been like in its day. Today seagulls wheel and shriek amid the gaunt bleak ruin that rises up from the beach, its lines now obscured by vines and weeds. All but two stately pillars, black with decay, cling to the crumbling structure. The second floor is gone, destroyed by fire in the 'Fifties when the decorative tent ceiling caught fire. Shattered glass and charred terra-cotta tiles lie in heaps amid the rubble that surrounds the stucco walls of the building that extends out along the water's edge. Leaning against an old water trough is a rusting sign that reads HARBORWOOD. Few people alive today recall the structure's colorful and infamous past.

THE MAIN ENTRANCE TO THE BOATHOUSE

Once considered the world's largest privately owned boathouse, it was built by the flamboyant movie mogul J. Stewart Blackton around 1914. In this waterside setting some of the grandest Hollywood-style parties took place. Everyone from Ziegfeld show-girls to would-be royalty to café society came by boat, then climbed the marble staircase that led to a massive ballroom on the second floor. Designed by Hoppin and Koen, the design took its inspiration from the classic seaside villas of Italy. Dozens of Palladian French doors opened out onto a spacious balustraded veranda with a sweeping view of the sound. Inside, a red and white circus-tented ceiling billowed in the soft sea breezes. A pair of massive fireplaces stood at each end of the room. Arranged in comfortable groupings were fawn-green Victorian wicker chairs and couches.

From the harbor, Blackton's hundred and fifty foot yacht would glide into the long narrow canal and enter a wide cavernous arch graced by a lion's head keystone at the top. Once inside, a pair of sharp-pointed iron gates would close behind it. Guard dogs, and even a lion, were kept chained on the property to keep out the curious. It is rumored that during the days of Prohibition the yacht was used for rum-running bootleg gin across the sound to Connecticut.

As grand as the boathouse was, Blackton was about to build his dream palace on a hill overlooking the property when disaster struck. When talking pictures took over Hollywood, many investors lost their fortunes. Blackton was one of them. He sold his yacht to make ends meet; his boathouse was closed and later sold. His plan to build a forty-room mansion came to an end, and he spent the remainder of his days living in the stucco caretaker's cottage nearby. His pet lion was sent to the Bronx Zoo.

BOATHOUSE RUINS IN 1984

THE MAIN SALON OVERLOOKING THE FORMAL GARDENS

MALMAISON

Tucked away amid an overgrown forest off a busy street in Brookville stands one of Long Island's best-kept secrets. A magnificent French château, painted villa pink, is practically hidden from view at the end of an alley of mountain laurel. The original Malmaison, built northwest of Paris during the middle ages, had at one time been owned by the Abbey of Saint Denis, and was used as a hospital for the incurably ill. It was completely renovated by Napoleon in 1799 for his beloved Empress Josephine. This modified American version was built in 1916.

One enters the estate through a large white wrought-iron gate which opens onto a spacious courtyard banked by a sixteen-foot stucco wall set with two niches that arch over a pair of life-size terra-cotta statues. The front façade bears the stamp of Napoleon's taste. A long "corps de logis" is broken up at the center by an extending balcony. At night, when you pull up the drive, the gate frames the house and your eye is drawn to that balcony, beyond which a magnificent chandelier can be seen shimmering like a fountain of diamonds. The Long Island showplace was designed by Ogden Codman for Walter Maynard, who during the summer of 1923 persuaded his friend Edith Wharton to stay on her last visit to the United States. The famed nineteenth-century writer, who spent most of her later days abroad, was in the country to receive a Doctorate of Letters from Yale University. She was said to have been so taken by Malmaison's authenticity, she stayed the summer drawing inspiration from its meticulously maintained Parisian-style gardens.

To the right of the entrance hall, a marble staircase soars like a graceful dove up three flights, then pauses on the main floor in an oval hallway set with arched niches, in which a pair of bisque statues stand. To the left of the hall, a pair of gilt-edged doors open onto the ballroom where rows of palladian glass doors in turn open onto the formal garden to the south and the entrance courtyard on the north side. Every detail of the room reflects an extravagance of romantic imagery: the gilt mirrors, the seven-foot Empire crystal chandelier, the priceless Louix XV gold piano, all under the gaze of dancing nymphs in the murals above the four entranceways. Appropriately, this grand salon is transformed once a year into a kind of dream fantasy, a room somewhere outside of time, when it becomes the setting for the annual Swan Ball hosted by the North Shore Preservation Society. While waltzing to music by Strauss, guests float about the room in mid-nineteenth-century dress, complete with voluminous layers of petticoats, hoop skirts, long white gloves, and feathered and jeweled headdresses. Victorian dance cards are signed by white-tie-and-tailed gents for the cotillion dances.

Outside, dozens of flaming torches bathe the gardens in an ethereal light. At the far end of the garden, swans glide on the still waters of a reflecting pool. In a distant corner of the garden stands a latticed arcade with a pair of wooden obelisks on either side. Though somewhat fallen to ruin, at one time the fourteen-foot trellis was painted fawn green and white and pink tea roses were trained to cascade in and around the graceful structure. Moving northward one crosses a wide expanse of lawn to a vast series of marble staircases framed by a pair of classic urns.

The rear veranda is supported by four white pillars that cast their shadows on the polished terrazzo floor below. Water trickles from a pair of bronze fish into a pink seashell basin. In days gone by, tea was served here each afternoon amid the Boston ferns and lavender hydrangeas.

The one room in the house where Napoleon's influence makes itself felt most powerfully is the library. The entire room was imported from France, and the rest of the house was designed in balanced proportion around it. The painted wood panels are of a rich brown, black, and burnt sienna color, and are painted in the attenuated Pompeiian manner. A wide decorative band running along the ceiling is decorated with hand-painted stags, elk, antelope, and deer. Empire-style bugle-bearing nymphs grace the main door, while richly carved garlands of roses and laurel act as handles for the doors of the built-in bookcases on one wall. A black marble mantel with a mirror rising up to the ceiling dominates the room. The brass and enamel chandelier is an exact replica of the one that graced Napoleon's library originally designed by Percier and Fontaine.

The dining room is a classic example of simple, graceful design, with balanced proportion and plain unadorned moldings. On the far south wall there is a picturesque twelve-foot mural of Empress Josephine stepping into a gondola, with a Roman-style love temple in the background. Originally there were four other murals; over the years they have been covered by layers of paint. To the left of the Louis XV marble mantel is a built-in three-sided glass case which holds a fine collection of Limoges china. Colorful scenes reflecting court life in the Louis XV era are embroidered in petit point panels on the twenty matching carved oak chairs that surround the dining room table.

MAIN ENTRANCE COURTYARD

A pair of Directoire wall brackets add rhythm and decorative relief to the otherwise simple nature of the room. Upstairs, a variety of charming bedroom suites done in the French style, some with Boiserie walls, are arranged along a wide central hall on the third floor.

A twentieth-century feature of the house built over the vast length of servants' quarters is a large theater on the second floor. This room contains a projection booth, movie screen, and a small stage. Today the house is no longer engulfed in English ivy, and the green and white striped awning that once shielded the rear terrace from the sun is gone. At the south end of the garden a more modern pool has replaced the round one with its colorful borders of perennials. No one knows what became of the splendid fountain that rose up from a tiny island of fossil coral, from which a pair of winged nymphs reached out to a huge swan from whose mouth a constant stream of water rose six feet. Yet, in this dwelling so far removed from the twentieth century, the magic lingers, and in the hushed stillness of the overgrown garden, it's as if the house remembers that Edith Wharton once stayed here.

Malmaison is owned by the noted architect John Maddocks.

EBBIN

Ebbin is a living monument to the survival of several Gold Coast estates that are enjoying a second heyday after the fall of so many of their neighbors. Sixteen years ago the house was near ruin after years of abandonment. The aristocratic manor house, built in 1916 by Mortimer Barnes, was designed by Thomas Harlan Ellett as a backdrop for one of the North Shore's most beautiful gardens. In a picturesque setting, the house sits high on a hilltop and follows the contours of the surrounding land.

Long before you reach the house, the eye is caught by a vast and unusual carriage house reminiscent of those found throughout the south of France and in Italy. The old-world building is attached to the main house through the medium of a "colombier" in the style of the "ferme du manoir" of provincial Europe. The carriage house, now covered in English ivy, is built of rough hard-burned local brick, the exterior walls laid

out to produce an irregular surface, then whitewashed with paint often used on light houses to create a weathered effect. The building is almost the length of a football field, and contains a cow barn, horse stables, hayloft, wagon shed, laundry room, workshop, dovecote, and enough space for almost a dozen cars. The north end is crowned by a French-style tower with a pigeon house at the top; below it are living quarters for servants. A spiral staircase begins at the basement level where an old pumping plant still exists, and a wide courtyard separates the main house from the stables. Ancient poplar trees run along a sixteen-foot wall that rises up to the level of the formal gardens. A pergola supported by stone pillars is shaded by rambling wisteria vines; in its day tea was served there on warm summer afternoons under the mantle of lavender blooms.

The front entrance to the house is guarded by a pair of marble nymphs, a more recent addition. Originally there were a pair of bronze peacocks mounting the pedestals at each end of the limestone balustrades. The French-style house has tall glass doors running along the entire main floor, most accentuated with wrought-iron balconys. A double staircase leads to the front entrance which overlooks the upper courtyard and drive. Arriving guests are received in a spacious entrance hall, where a carved oak table supports a large Chinese fishbowl.

Ebbin is a house designed for entertaining, as its imported French ballroom to the left of the hall amply demonstrates. Its two-hundred-year-old Fontainebleau floors creak appropriately when you walk across them. The Louis XIV mantel, with its built-in mirror, reflects a gracious room decorated with gilt Louis XVI furniture covered with red silk damask fabric. A huge concert grand piano dominates the south wall, and is in constant use. Ebbin's present owners, Thomas and Alicia Zizzo, entertain often, their Sunday candlelight musicales recalling a life-style reminiscent of the last century. Alicia Zizzo is the world-renowned concert pianist, and she has added to the house's fine collection of antiques on her travels about the globe on concert tours. Mr. Zizzo, an equal contributor to the arts, has sung with the National Grand Opera company.

An oak-paneled library at the center of the house is filled with rare books on art and music. The entire south wall was designed to open, allowing the formal gardens to appear part of the room itself. A pair of enormous French glass doors receed into the walls by means of a hydraulic mechanism. On the second floor all the bedrooms have marble fireplaces and French doors that open onto balconies overlooking the formal gardens, at the center of which is a round reflecting pool enhanced by a bronze fountain. Another rare feature of the house is the charming breakfast room, with its black and green terrazzo floor. At one time a huge aviary extended out onto the flagstone terrace and into the gardens beyond. During the summer months colorful exotic birds sang and flew among trees that rose up some fourteen feet to the iron mesh ceiling. A multi-tiered fountain doubled as a birdbath.

Today Ebbin is one of those rare North Shore mansions that stands as a living monument to the determination, enterprise, and cleverness of its proud owners whose efforts have seen to it that it will endure for decades to come.

ENTRANCE TO THE STABLE AND THE PIDGEON HOUSE

THE FORMAL GARDENS

ENTRANCE FOYER

THE MAIN SALON

THE DINING ROOM

DECORATIVE FISH NETTING SUPPORTED BY ANCHORS, INDOOR TENNIS COURT

HAROLD PRATT'S
INDOOR TENNIS COURT

PLAY PALACES

The Pratts, Mackays and Whitneys referred to the "play palaces" more modestly as playhouses. They were in essence sports complexes and casinos. Tennis under glass was another pastime of the rich. Inside the ivy-draped walls of the huge clay courts themselves, many of these playhouses were complete with indoor heated pools, steam baths, saunas, squash courts, bowling alleys, shooting ranges with moving targets, billiard rooms, bars, gymnasiums, dressing and guest rooms. One had a gambling casino hidden behind a secret paneled wall. Several playhouses had their private movie theatre, balcony for an orchestra, and ballroom to hold hundreds of guests. Built during the 'Twenties and early 'Thirties, they were designed by top architects, James O'Connors in particular, and were in keeping with the style of the main houses on the estates. The playhouses are best spotted from the air: their blue glass roofs are unmistakable, since they are the largest of the buildings found on any estate.

At one time there were about thirty of these playhouses, and out of that number more than twenty are still being used. With tennis becoming one of America's favorite pastimes, these buildings stand a better chance of surviving the bulldozer than many other types of estate buildings. Each tennis house had its resident pro and caretakers who groomed the courts and hand watered the lush cascading ivy that clug to the sides of the walls to provide oxygen for the players. Structurally, the basic design of the courts was similar, usually measuring 156 feet long by 80 feet wide, with the ceilings towering up some 60 feet or more. Hundreds of 350-watt bulbs lit the courts to simulate daylight at night. In the small village of Oyster Bay Cove, a resident groundskeeper had to notify Lilco in advance of turning the court lights on, to prevent an overload.

Many of the fabled parties were held in the tennis courts because of their size. The wedding of Helena McCann, daughter of F. W. Woolworth, to Winston Guest in the 'Thirties was said to be one of the most lavish. A dance hall was set up in the court, and an entire train load of tropical palm trees was brought up from Florida. The hundreds of trees were then set up in huge tubs and placed around the room. Trellises covered with gardenias and tiny lights decorated the walls. Paul Whiteman's band, who played for Rudy Vallee, played from a stage that had been set up for the evening. As many as eighteen guest rooms would house the overflow of guests from the main house.

THE INDOOR SWIMMING POOL ON THE FORMER DODGE SLOANE ESTATE

THE LATTINGTOWN TENNIS CLUB, FORMERLY ON THE DODGE SLOANE ESTATE

It is interesting how each owner expressed his or her taste in a variety of ways. One court was lined with French treillage on the walls. John Hay Whitney's court at Greentree in Manhasset is lined with deer and moose heads, while Mrs. Harold Erving Pratt, in keeping with her husband's great love of the sea, chose to drape the walls with miles of fishnets held in place by ornamental anchors. Dozens of American wooden Indians stood watch along the borders of the court on the Watson Webb estate in Old Westbury. The indoor pool is entered through a delicate wrought iron gate decorated with iron flowers, butterflies, birds and bees. The theme is continued throughout the room with hand painted murals of an English country flower garden. In most playhouses, much attention was given to the decorating of the adjoining rooms and guest suites; murals painted by famous artists of the day were a popular way of dealing with the spacious walls. I am told that one dressing room had an all-glass floor where one could look down and watch tropical fish swimming around and about the coral and shells below.

The Woodward playhouse was one of the showplaces, with its fine collection of art treasures and tapestries, built-in pipe organ and leaded stained glass windows. Perhaps the most spectacular of these play palaces was Oak Point, former estate of Harrison Williams, who made millions in utilities holding companies. It stood on a high bluff commanding a magnificent view of Long Island Sound. The high steel-framed, glass-domed complex with its pillared rotunda entrance was the ultimate in luxury. It housed a beautiful pool where several live peacocks were free to strut and roam around. The pool converted into a dance floor when covered by a hydraulically operated floor. An Art Deco lounge had a stately series of wide-arched paneled walls soaring up to a vaulted ceiling with metallic silver draperies. Two circular stairways led from an entrance hall down to another lounge where colorful murals were painted by the talented Spanish artist José Sert. The sports house, as the Williams' called it, was a splendid stage for Mrs. Harrison Williams, a celebrated toast of high society. She was a woman of great beauty, voted the best-dressed woman in the world. It is said that she had seven Rolls Royces, one for each day of the week, with a footman and chauffeur in livery matching the color of the car.

Before World War II, the Williams' maintained five estates both here and in Europe, and employed a staff of 130 servants. Forty-five of that number ran their 275-foot yacht *Warrior*. Fifty men tended to her fabulous gardens that surrounded the Playhouse and the huge Georgian manor that stood nearby. The willow garden, with its radial reflecting pond, overlooked a Chinese rock garden that is said to have cost some $100,000 to construct. Dissatisfied with its layout, I'm told, she had it leveled and redone at again the same cost. There were also endless vistas of well-tended lawns, a yew garden, cascading roses over walled-in gardens, and endless brick paths surrounded by masses of lilac trees so high that in spring the sky seemed almost swallowed up by the fragrant purple blossoms.

In 1950, the main house was torn down. It had become a burden following the war, when most of the servants had been drafted or went to work in defense plants leaving many of the estates high and dry. Mona and her husband decided to make the playhouse their home. Because she loved plants and flowers more than tennis, she had the court transformed into what had to be the largest aviary in the world. Hundreds of tropical birds flew about the palms and flowering plants that were brought in from all over the world. Many were gifts from friends. A half-trellis gazebo set off one end of the room, while a formal reflecting pool graced the center. Mr. Williams would sit for hours with his binoculars watching the birds flutter about, from the balcony, while Mona tended to the care of her prized orchids and camellias. So fond was she of gardenias that in a popular fashion magazine of the time it was said that she ate a gardenia each day with tea.

When Harrison Williams died, Oak Point was all but abandoned. The caretaker remained in the cottage, but it was a losing battle to keep out the vandals, who climbed past the barbed wire fence that ran along the cliffs on the water side. In 1968, all was lost in a disastrous fire set by vandals, leaving only a steel skeleton frame of the aviary court to remind us of departed glories. In time, Mona remarried and is now the Countesss Von Bismark. Flowers are still her passion and she is said to have one of the most beautiful gardens in Italy.

Many of the surviving tennis courts are thriving very much as in the old days, though now the taxes run about $8,000 a year, the 20,000 gallon tanks run about $14,000 to keep filled, electric bills run close to $5,000 per year, not to mention maintenance and gardening costs. The former Cornelius Vanderbilt Whitney court is now the popular Old Westbury Country Club, though the tiled indoor pool is covered

TROPICAL ARBORETUM, THE FORMER TENNIS COURT ADJOINING THE INDOOR
SWIMMING POOL. THE HARRISON WILLIAMS ESTATE

over and the room used for paddle tennis. In recent years, the ivy was taken down, making it easier to maintain the walls. The upper level lobby with its marble fireplace and wood beamed ceiling is still a favorite spot for guests to watch the games.

John Teel Pratt's compound now serves as the YMCA gym for local residents of Glen Cove. There are several indoor courts in the Lattingtown area. Some are privately owned and maintained as exclusive clubs like the former Isabel Dodge Sloane playhouse, now owned and run by tennis pro Bud de Gonzague. The sister of Huntington Hartford, Josephine Hartford Douglas, built her own indoor tennis court when she was refused a reservation one afternoon at the Piping Rock Club with the explanation that it was all booked up. The walls of the adjoining swimming pool were gaily painted by a famous Russian artist—with polar bears, moose, buffalo and flamingoes all engaged in erotic activities. Tennis greats Bill Tilden and Billie Jean King came here to play the game and attend the fabulous parties that took place here. Even with the main house gone, a long underground tunnel runs from where the house was to the still flourishing court. It was built to avoid running through the rain.

THE PRATT STABLES AND SPORTS CASINO, WELWYN

WELWYN, THE PIER

Not far from the former home of Theodore Roosevelt is the Mather tennis complex, one of the largest, and the only round high-domed court on the Island. It can be seen for miles around at night as it overlooks Oyster Bay Harbor, its all-glass roof a blaze of light. Clarence Mackay was one of the first to build a sporting casino in 1909. The all-marble building had a heated pool, bowling alley, gym, rifle range and theatre. It, too, was vandalized and burnt to the ground in the 'Fifties.

Welwyn, former home of Harold Erving Pratt, its court no longer used, retains a haunting quality about it. Its soft mottled green walls and ruined clay floor take on a different character. The rotting fish nets around the walls begin to sag with time, and the guest rooms on the upper level have not seen a fresh coat of paint in thirty years. Still, there is a purity about that I find pleasing, a quiet dignity that comes from its total isolation in time. In the ladies' dressing room the pink floral chintz is still crisp on the boudoir chairs that have been pushed off to one corner. Several Art Deco mirrors hang on the walls and the window shades have yellowed with age. An old white iron weighing scale stands in the corner of the small room, but for all its lack of glamour you can still feel here the magic that seemed to stop back in the 'Sixties, when many of the last of the great houses fell to their doom. The only sound that could be heard when I visited there last was the water dripping rhythmically from a crack in the glass ceiling, falling sixty feet onto the damp floor below, recalling a once-vivid drama of yet another fading ruin.

Joe Farrell, who now has deep dark sombre eyes, graying hair, and, with pipe in hand, wears a long Harris tweed overcoat, remembers the golden era with remarkable clarity and pride. Now in his seventies, he once brushed shoulders with kings, taught the Pratts, Whitneys, Astors, the Prince of Wales, the Vanderbilts, and Morgans to play the game of tennis; he won top national tennis championships and attended just about every ball, banquet, coming out party, hunt tea, horse show opening and polo game.

Though he was never a member of Piping Rock nor listed in the social register,

WEATHER VANE
ON THE PLAY HOUSE
OF HAROLD PRATT

241

LOUNGE OVERLOOKING INDOOR TENNIS COURT, H. P. WHITNEY ESTATE

he lived the life as well as any blue-blooded tycoon of that fabled day. He took Mrs. Harrison Williams dancing, and recalls, "She was the most beautiful and gracious woman I ever met. . . . We called her 'Slim'—she floated across the dance floor like a vision of grace in her gossamer chiffon gowns."

When Long Island's elite traveled around Europe, Joe went with them as their private tennis coach. He played tennis with King George of England and King Olaf of Sweden, who gave him a set of gold cufflinks with the country's coat of arms on it, a gift he still prizes. He was a guest at Buckingham Palace where he claims there was "Great service at the old place, you couldn't walk down the hall without the footmen and chamber maids jumping on you."

A man of many talents, he became a pilot and flew from estate to estate on Long Island: there would be a game at Otto Kahn's 100-room château in the morning, then on to the Pratt Oval in Glen Cove for a round at Harold Erving Pratt's indoor court, Welwyn, then off again to land in the polo field or race track or just about any open space to give a lesson to Harold S. Vanderbilt. In Joe's words, "He was really something, could only play the game while singing the Merry Widow Waltz. He said the rhythm of the song helped him concentrate and keep in time." Joe said, "I taught them all, and was always welcome at their parties."

He was the only one allowed to attend Mrs. Payson's fabulous affairs without a costume. "Her parties were the greatest," he said, "You can't imagine how beautiful everything was then; anybody who was anybody was there—Billy Paley, Alister Martin,

242

UPSTAIRS BATHROOM LEADING DOWN TO INDOOR SWIMMING POOL
OF FORMER DODGE SLOANE ESTATE

THE HARRY PAYNE WHITNEY PLAYHOUSE INCLUDED TENNIS AND SQUASH COURTS, A SWIMMING POOL, BOWLING ALLEYS AND OTHER FACILITIES

Jock Whitney, John Schiff, the Morgans. . . . Everyone was young and gay, people would end up in the pool, it was all great fun. There was always someplace to go, some dinner party or dance, the polo games, Meadowbrook hunts—Arthur Loew every Sunday would show movies for his friends in his private theater at Pembroke, or we'd go skeet shooting at Marshall Field's, or clamming off the Sound. It was funny, but with all that money and servants people had in those days, some of the best times we had were catching fish along the rocks off Oak Point and cooking them right there in the sand with no silver to cut them with, and eating them in our hands.

"But oh, those great yachts that would sail by. I remember being on the *Corsair*, almost 300 feet long, and the Williams' boat *Warrior*. Like floating islands, they were complete with gold fixtures, and imported paneling, and stewards waiting on you hand and foot. There was great style then, everyone had to know how to dress in those days. Knowing the rules became a part of you, you always knew what was expected and played by the rules."

Mr. Farrell did in fact know every one of the 500 or so manor houses in great detail. At some point in his varied career he got into building tennis courts, and swimming pools. They were among the most elaborate I've ever seen. We spent several days driving around the North Shore visiting his old friends, and yes, everyone knew Joe Farrell. At one point it became heartbreaking for him as we toured Old Westbury. He said, "Turn in there, I want you to see the old Garvan place, and next to it is old Henry Carnegie Phipps' marble villa Wheatley House. . . ." I had to say, "But it's gone."

Mr. Farrell in shocked disbelief said, "My God, but it can't be, it just can't be, there is nothing to take its place!"

OTTO KAHN'S CASTLE

Just about a mile off the busy Jericho Turnpike, in Woodbury, the land suddenly rises to reveal a breathtaking vision of Otto Kahn's fairytale castle. The home, built with a monumentality never before equaled on the North Shore, was constructed in 1921 by the flamboyant banking financier and railroad baron. His architect was William Adams Delano. Two years were spent artificially constructing a mountain on the five-hundred-acre estate, that would make it the highest point on the Island. With one hundred and twenty-six rooms, and an equal number of servants, the palatial château became the second largest private home in the United States.

Otto Kahn, a legend now, was born in 1867 in Mannheim, Germany, son of a banker whose family shared an appreciation for the arts and music. At the age of twenty-five, Kahn came to America and joined Speyer & Co., a small banking firm. With his marriage to Adele Wolff in 1896, Kahn was then welcomed as a partner in Kuhn, Loeb & Co., a banking firm owned by Abraham Wolff, the girl's father. Kahn's endless

OTTO KAHN ESTATE

energy and drive soon had him tackling problems the firm had considered hopeless. He won international acclaim with his foreign economic and humanitarian activities in the First World War. When the 'Twenties began, Kahn, though in his fifties, became one of the most active men in the country. The press often called him "the King of New York," and at one point he was director, or regarded as the chairman of, over seventy organizations.

A great lover of the arts and music like his family before him, he also found time to literally create the Metropolitan Opera Company with his boundless energy and financial backing, and went on to introduce and sponsor many of its stars, including Stanislavski, Caruso, Pavlova, and the Moscow Art Theater. At his great home in Cold Spring Harbor he staged some of the country's most celebrated parties. Guest lists often included penniless bohemians, members of the clergy, kings, socialites, actors, boisterous muscians, and Ziegfeld girls. The grand dining hall seated a record-breaking two hundred guests, with Kahn at the far end, surrounded always by his dachshunds on even the most formal occasions.

ENTRANCE TO THE OTTO KAHN ESTATE WAS THROUGH THE GATEWAY TO THE RIGHT

The entrance drive to the house was bordered by red cedars, terminating in a huge courtyard paved with cobblestones from old New York streets. One is immediately drawn to the entertaining peaked rooftops, whose slates are of varying sizes, giving a wave-like effect. The French château follows the shape of a long plateau; a formal sunken garden stretches from the south side between allees of trees. In Otto Kahn's day it was one of the most breathtaking gardens of the Le Notre style; the geometric forms (parterre), usually of grass, were all of water which reflected the sky and fountains. Also found on the estate were a rose garden and a Dutch garden, a high ten-foot formally hedged garden used for playing croquet, endless rows of greenhouses, rambling stables, a nine hole golf course, and as a romantic note, a marble-pillared love temple.

With the death of Kahn in 1934, the house became empty for a time, and was then used as a rest home for sanitation workers. Today the once-magnificent home is known as Eastern Military Academy and over the years has been subjected to assaults and gross architectural changes made to conform with military demands. The formal reflecting gardens have been replaced by army barracks. Split levels now mar the once unobstructed view of the harbor, the great dining hall is now a grimly painted gymnasium, and Army tanks plow daily through the former lawns and surrounding woodlands. Students may come here to learn military tactics, but they'll surely have to go somewhere else to learn about beauty, and respect for the architectural achievements of greater men, who will not be passing this way again.

247

IN THE FORMAL GARDEN

MILL NECK MANOR

Robert L. Dodge

Among the finest surviving examples of English Tudor architecture is the former home of Mr. and Mrs. Robert L. Dodge. The forty-room mansion, built around 1925, stands atop a rolling hill, and has a breathtaking view of Long Island Sound and Connecticut. Stone Gothic gables, and hip roofs recall the feeling of many a haunting tale. A heavy fifteenth century oak door is sheltered under a stone portico entrance. The interiors of the great hall and other adjoining rooms acquire their rich atmosphere from the oak paneled walls. The rooms are shadowy with light coming in through the leaded glass windows, set with colorful stained glass medallions.

249

Mrs. Dodge sent for German artisans to sculpture the patterned plaster ceiling, from which Renaissance chandeliers hung throughout the house. Many of the fireplaces are of sandstone and originally graced castles in England, France and Germany. The rooms, which remain uniform in style and character, are enlivened with paintings, screens, tapestries, brocades, Persian rugs and heavy bronze andirons. An outstanding feature of the house is the stained glass window above the stairway landing, a masterpiece done by L. C. Tiffany. It was commissioned by Mrs. Dodge and depicts five famous plays by Shakespeare: The Tempest, Hamlet, Macbeth, Romeo and Juliet, and The Merry Wives of Windsor. Below it, a long fifteenth century cathedral pew conceals a radiator cover.

Mill Neck Manor's special claim to fame rests on the elegance and ethereal quality of the formal gardens. English boxwood is carefully clipped in a radial pattern to represent a sundial. A fountain at one end originally threw water high into the air. Rows of classic urns border the garden, and at each corner of the garden stands a stone temple with statuary set in niches. In spring, the setting is radiant with the glow of pink Japanese cherry blossoms that surround a towering stone love temple. Since 1950, Mill Neck Manor has been used by the Lutheran School for the Deaf. The Tudor stables have been converted into office space, the main house is used for classrooms. There have been some changes on the estate and the rich furnishings have been sold off, but the charm and grace of the setting will remain for many years to come.

THIS TIFFANY DESIGNED STAINED GLASS WINDOW DEPICTS FIVE PLAYS BY SHAKESPEARE

Bibliography

American Adaptation of the French Chateau, 1917

The American Architect, May 5, 1929, Harrison Williams Sports House

The American Architect, Sept. 17, 1919, Pembroke, Delano & Aldrich

Community, April 28, 1966, F. W. Woolworth

Barr Farrell, *American Estates and Gardens,* 1904

Fortune, June 1932, W. D. Guthrie

Sheldon George, *Artistic Country Seats, Types of Recent American Villa & Cottage Arch.*

Holiday, Oct. 1948 The North Shore

Holiday, Sept. 1958

Homes for People in Suburb and Country. Villas & Mansions

Robert Koch, *L. C. Tiffany, Rebel in Glass*

Life, July 22, 1946, The North Shore, Clark Estate, W. R. Coe

Life, Nov. 1955 William Woodward case, Cleveland Armory

Locust Valley Leader, The Fabled Past, Oak Point—A Tale of Bygone Days, 1968

Long Island Press, April 22, 1962, W. C. Bird

Ray W. Moger, Roslyn Then & Now, Mackay Estate

Price C. Matlock, *Transplanted Architecture*

Monograph of the Work of McKim Mead & White 1879-1915, Harbor Hill,
    Architectural Book Publishing Co., 1915

Newsday, Moments Preserved by John Handler, 1975-76

Newsday, Nov. 15, 1965, Whitney, Greentree

Newsday, Dec. 1, 1965, Estates & Their Story

Newsday, May 21, 1977, C. Z. Guest

Newsday, Tennis Under Glass, Dec. 8, 1977

The New York Times, Sun. Sept. 7, 1924, Guest List, Harbor Hill Party

New York Times, Dec. 8, 1957, Mill Neck Manor, Otto Kahn, J. P. Morgan,
    C. Pratt

On the Sound, April 1974

Augusta O. Patterson, *American Homes of Today,* 1924

Herbert H. L. Pratt, *American Country Houses of Today,* 1915

INDEX